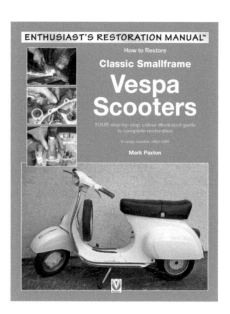

ENTHUSIAST'S RESTORATION MANUAL™

How to Restore

Classic Smallframe

Vespa
Scooters

YOUR step-by-step colour illustrated guide
to complete restoration

V-range models 1963-1986

Mark Paxton

T0386285

Other great scooter and motorcycle books from Veloce:

SpeedPro Series
Harley-Davidson Evolution Engines, How to Build & Power Tune (Hammill)
Motorcycle-engined Racing Cars, How to Build (Pashley)

Workshop Pro Series
Car electrical and electronic systems (Edgar)
Setting up a home car workshop (Edgar)

RAC Handbooks
Caring for your scooter – How to maintain & service your 49cc to 125cc twist & go scooter (Fry)
How your motorcycle works – Your guide to the components & systems of modern motorcycles (Henshaw)
Motorcycles – A first-time-buyer's guide (Henshaw)

Enthusiast's Restoration Manual Series
Beginner's Guide to Classic Motorcycle Restoration, The (Burns)
Classic Large Frame Vespa Scooters, How to Restore (Paxton)
Ducati Bevel Twins 1971 to 1986 (Falloon)
Classic Off-road Motorcycles, How to Restore (Burns)
Honda CX500 & CX650, How to restore – YOUR step-by-step colour illustrated guide to complete restoration (Burns)
Honda Fours, How to restore – YOUR step-by-step colour illustrated guide to complete restoration (Burns)
Kawasaki Z1, Z/KZ900 & Z/KZ1000, How to restore (Rooke)
Triumph Trident T150/T160 & BSA Rocket III, How to Restore (Rooke)
Yamaha FS1-E, How to Restore (Watts)

Essential Buyer's Guide Series
BMW Boxer Twins (Henshaw)
BMW GS (Henshaw)
BSA 350, 441 & 500 Singles (Henshaw)
BSA 500 & 650 Twins (Henshaw)
BSA Bantam (Henshaw)
Ducati Bevel Twins (Falloon)
Ducati Desmodue Twins (Falloon)
Ducati Desmoquattro Twins – 851, 888, 916, 996, 998, ST4 1988 to 2004 (Falloon)
Harley-Davidson Big Twins (Henshaw)
Hinckley Triumph triples & fours 750, 900, 955, 1000, 1050, 1200 – 1991-2009 (Henshaw)
Honda CBR FireBlade (Henshaw)
Honda CBR600 Hurricane (Henshaw)
Honda SOHC Fours 1969-1984 (Henshaw)
Kawasaki Z1 & Z900 (Orritt)
Moto Guzzi 2-valve big twins (Falloon)
Norton Commando (Henshaw)
Piaggio Scooters – all modern two-stroke & four-stroke automatic models 1991 to 2016 (Willis)
Royal Enfield Bullet (Henshaw)
Triumph 350 & 500 Twins (Henshaw)
Triumph Bonneville (Henshaw)
Triumph Thunderbird, Trophy & Tiger (Henshaw)
Velocette 350 & 500 Singles 1946 to 1970 (Henshaw)
Vespa Scooters – Classic 2-stroke models 1960-2008 (Paxton)

Those Were The Days ... Series
Café Racer Phenomenon, The (Walker)
Drag Bike Racing in Britain – From the mid '60s to the mid '80s (Lee)

Auto-Graphics Series
Lambretta Li Series Scooters (Sparrow)

Biographies
Chris Carter at Large – Stories from a lifetime in motorcycle racing (Carter & Skelton)
Edward Turner – The Man Behind the Motorcycles (Clew)
Jim Redman – 6 Times World Motorcycle Champion: The Autobiography (Redman)
'Sox' – Gary Hocking – the forgotten World Motorcycle Champion (Hughes)

General
BMW Boxer Twins 1970-1995 Bible, The (Falloon)
BMW Cafe Racers (Cloesen)
BMW Custom Motorcycles – Choppers, Cruisers, Bobbers, Trikes & Quads (Cloesen)
Bonjour – Is this Italy? (Turner)
British 250cc Racing Motorcycles (Pereira)
British Café Racers (Cloesen)
British Custom Motorcycles – The Brit Chop – choppers, cruisers, bobbers & trikes (Cloesen)
BSA Bantam Bible, The (Henshaw)
BSA Motorcycles – the final evolution (Jones)
Ducati 750 Bible, The (Falloon)
Ducati 750 SS 'round-case' 1974, The Book of the (Falloon)
Ducati 860, 900 and Mille Bible, The (Falloon)
Ducati Monster Bible (New Updated & Revised Edition), The (Falloon)
Ducati Story, The – 6th Edition (Falloon)
Ducati 916 (updated edition) (Falloon)
Essential Guide to Driving in Europe, The (Parish)
Fine Art of the Motorcycle Engine, The (Peirce)
Franklin's Indians (Sucher/Pickering/Diamond/Havelin)
From Crystal Palace to Red Square – A Hapless Biker's Road to Russia (Turner)
Funky Mopeds (Skelton)
India - The Shimmering Dream (Reisch/Falls (translator)
Italian Cafe Racers (Cloesen)
Italian Custom Motorcycles (Cloesen)
Japanese Custom Motorcycles – The Nippon Chop – Chopper, Cruiser, Bobber, Trikes and Quads (Cloesen)
Kawasaki Triples Bible, The (Walker)
Kawasaki Z1 Story, The (Sheehan)
Laverda Twins & Triples Bible 1968-1986 (Falloon)
Little book of trikes, the (Quellin)
Mike the Bike – Again (Macauley)
Mini Cooper – The Real Thing! (Tipler)
Mini Minor to Asia Minor (West)
Mitsubishi Lancer Evo, The Road Car & WRC Story (Long)
Moto Guzzi Sport & Le Mans Bible, The (Falloon)
The Moto Guzzi Story – 3rd Edition (Falloon)
Motorcycle Apprentice (Cakebread)
Motorcycle GP Racing in the 1960s (Pereira)
Motorcycle Racing with the Continental Circus 1920-1970 (Pereira)
Motorcycle Road & Racing Chassis Designs (Noakes)
Motorcycling in the '50s (Clew)
MV Agusta Fours, The book of the classic (Falloon)
Norton Commando Bible – All models 1968 to 1978 (Henshaw)
Off-Road Giants! (Volume 1) – Heroes of 1960s Motorcycle Sport (Westlake)
Off-Road Giants! (Volume 2) – Heroes of 1960s Motorcycle Sport (Westlake)
Off-Road Giants! (Volume 3) – Heroes of 1960s Motorcycle Sport (Westlake)
Peking to Paris 2007 (Young)
Racing Line – British motorcycle racing in the golden age of the big single (Guntrip)
The Red Baron's Ultimate Ducati Desmo Manual (Cabrera Choclán)
Roads with a View – England's greatest views and how to find them by road (Corfield)
Runways & Racers (O'Neil)
Scooters & Microcars, The A-Z of Popular (Dan)
Scooter Lifestyle (Grainger)
Scooter Mania! – Recollections of the Isle of Man International Scooter Rally (Jackson)
Suzuki Motorcycles - The Classic Two-stroke Era (Long)
Triumph Bonneville Bible (59-83) (Henshaw)
Triumph Bonneville!, Save the – The inside story of the Meriden Workers' Co-op (Rosamond)
Triumph Motorcycles & the Meriden Factory (Hancox)
Triumph Speed Twin & Thunderbird Bible (Woolridge)
Triumph Tiger Cub Bible (Estall)
Triumph Trophy Bible (Woolridge)
Triumph TR6 (Kimberley)
TT Talking – The TT's most exciting era – As seen by Manx Radio TT's lead commentator 2004-2012 (Lambert)
Velocette Motorcycles – MSS to Thruxton – Third Edition (Burris)
Vespa – The Story of a Cult Classic in Pictures (Uhlig)
Vincent Motorcycles: The Untold Story since 1946 (Guyony & Parker)

www.veloce.co.uk

First published in June 2013 reprinted August 2018 by Veloce Publishing Limited, Veloce House, Parkway Farm Business Park, Middle Farm Way, Poundbury, Dorchester DT1 3AR, England. Tel +44 (0)1305 260068 / Fax 01305 250479 / e-mail info@ veloce.co.uk / web www.veloce.co.uk or www.velocebooks.com.ISBN: 978-1-787114-08-1 UPC: 6-36847-01408-7 © 2018 Mark Paxton and Veloce Publishing. All rights reserved. With the exception of quoting brief passages for the purpose of review, no part of this publication may be recorded, reproduced or transmitted by any means, including photocopying, without the written permission of Veloce Publishing Ltd. Throughout this book logos, model names and designations, etc, have been used for the purposes of identification, illustration and decoration. Such names are the property of the trademark holder as this is not an official publication. Readers with ideas for automotive books, or books on other transport or related hobby subjects, are invited to write to the editorial director of Veloce Publishing at the above address. British Library Cataloguing in Publication Data – A catalogue record for this book is available from the British Library. Typesetting, design and page make-up all by Veloce Publishing Ltd on Apple Mac. Printed and bound by CPI Group (UK) Ltd, Croydon, CR0 4YY.

How to Restore

Classic Smallframe

Vespa
Scooters

YOUR step-by-step colour illustrated guide
to complete restoration

V-range models 1963-1986

Mark Paxton

Veloce

Contents

CONTENTS

Introduction

By the end of the 1950s it was obvious that the scooter market was shrinking, as more and more people were able to afford the relative luxury of a car. The arrival of the Fiat 500 and the Mini added fashionable style to the appeal of four wheels, so Piaggio, like the other scooter manufacturers, needed to find new customers to take up the slack. The choice was fairly simple in the end: legislation changes on the Continent allowed 14-year-olds to ride 50cc machines without a licence or insurance, and as teenagers were enjoying the benefits of the economic boom along with their parents, there was money to be spent, and so the Vespa Smallframe was born. It was an immediate and enduring success, not only thanks to its obvious appeal to young people, but it quickly became apparent that the compact dimensions mated to a highly tuneable motor made for a very attractive combination. It was a long-lived design, surfacing in 1963 and continuing in some European markets, Germany, for example (but not the UK), until 1986. And even then the story wasn't over, as demand in Japan saw the scooter resurface for one final flourish in the early 1990s. A few were imported to Germany as the 50 Revival, and some appeared in other markets, but not as official Piaggio products.

Do some research into model variations before buying your Smallframe, as some parts are harder to source and are more expensive than others.

Smallframe ownership today is no less enjoyable, the scooters have survived in good numbers, and are supported by enthusiastic clubs and specialist dealers. Many have found their way to the UK from Italy and Spain to help meet booming demand, and restoration projects can be easily found. Prices are on the rise, though, making the amount required to resurrect one slightly less of a financial disaster than with most two wheelers.

CHASSIS NUMBERS

The main frame number is stamped into the top of the recessed lip where the engine cover closes. Additionally, depending on the market the scooter was originally destined for, there may be a pressed alloy plate riveted near the fuel tap lever. The number comprises a model code, which includes the letter T designating a frame, followed by a star then a four- to six-digit number, then another star.

Model	Code	Year
50 N	V5A1T	1963-1971
50 S	V5SA1T	1963-1984
50 L	V5A1T	1966-1970
50 R	V5A1T	1969-1983
50 Special	V5A2T	1969-1982
50 Special	V5B1T	1972-1985
50 Special	V5B3T	1975-1983

90	V9A1T	1963-1984
V100	V9B1T	1978-1984
125 Nuevo	VMA1T	1965-1967
Primavera	VMA2T	1967-1983
ET3	VMB 1T	1976-1983

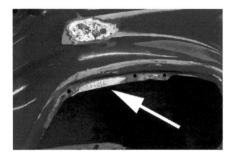

The frame number is stamped into the metal lip where the engine lid closes.

ENGINE NUMBERS

The engine code and number are stamped into the back of the engine next to the oil filler hole. This too will have a model code as above, but with the letter M replacing the T, followed by a number of four to six digits between two stars. There are numerous sites on the internet where the frame and engine numbers can be cross-referenced to double-check the provenance of your scooter.

The engine number is stamped into this flat casting next to the oil filler hole at the back of the motor.

PARTS

Unfortunately, parts quality is a major issue for restorers, and some care must be exercised when laying out your hard-earned cash. The best solution is to keep as many bits of the original scooter as can be salvaged. This may not initially seem cost-effective, as so many of the new parts are offered at attractive prices, but, in the long term, may prove the most economic. Always examine parts before purchase, and for that reason it will always be better to deal with your local scooter shop rather than buying blind off the internet. The good news is that virtually everything is available for your scooter, right down to the most obscure fittings, and all at reasonable prices compared to more recent vehicles. Smallframes have a massive following in mainland Europe, and suppliers there are actively involved in remanufacturing bits as original supplies dry up.

USING THIS BOOK

This volume makes no pretence at being a comprehensive workshop guide for every variant of Smallframe Vespa made. Instead, it seeks to cover major tasks in some detail, and should be used in conjunction with a traditional manual, and, perhaps more importantly, a copy of the parts book for your particular model. These books are freely available online or in paper form from parts suppliers.

The contents are a guide to renovation, restoration and repair, some of which encourages the use of non-standard parts. If you intend a complete rebuild to the original factory specifications then it would be wise to invest in the relevant volume in the *Vespa Tecnica* series Books 2 and 3 cover the Smallframe period and show the scooters in their original state. They are expensive, though, and if you decide you need Volume 6 with its included paint swatches, be prepared for a wallet-busting experience.

All the work shown here has been done by the author, as there really is no substitute for personal experience in order to get a feel for the effort, skill, or nerve jangling frustration involved in the restoration process. The techniques outlined may differ from those advocated by some, but they all work.

Gather as much information as you can find about your chosen scooter. It will all help during the restoration process.

This scooter is the subject machine for this book. Its engine was originally a pile of bits in a box, but the scooter ended up looking like this by using the techniques contained within these pages.

Tuning has been ignored in the main as the scope for making your Smallframe go quicker is vast, as long as that desire is matched by an equally limitless source of cash. A few basic updates have been included, though, which could make the day-to-day use of your old Vespa more pleasurable. It's probably best to read the book through completely to get a feel for the process before diving into your particular restoration. On occasions, the picture sequence may show parts, fitted or missing, which may not have been covered in the text to that point, this is due to the fact that there are many ways to rebuild an engine, for example, so it's best to stick with the procedure laid out in the text until you have developed your own preferences.

PROJECT MANAGEMENT

The whole restoration process will be a juggling act between the conflicting forces of time, money and ability; the eventual proportions differing with each individual restorer. All the skills needed to renovate your Smallframe can be acquired by most people, but whether you have the time or inclination to develop them is a different matter.

Vespas can easily be broken down into large sub-assemblies, which can then be dealt with individually. Use a digital camera to record the process, as the pictures will jog your memory later as you struggle to remember where a cable ran or if a washer had been fitted. A note pad is a good idea as well, to list parts which need replacing.

The main thing with any restoration is to try and maintain progress, however small; once momentum is lost things stagnate, and it's difficult to recover the initial enthusiasm. Just take a look at the number of unfinished projects that are offered for sale.

TOOLS

There are only a few specialist tools that are required during the restoration, and these are mentioned in the text. They are all relatively inexpensive, and if you only intend doing one scooter they can always be sold on again afterwards. Frame repairs will mean access to a welder, and for paint application a compressor and gun. Even DIY models are a considerable investment, but will save money in the longer term. Hand tools should be of decent quality. Not many are needed so buy the best you can afford; it's much better to fork out on a good ratchet and a handful of quality sockets than on a giant set filled with sizes you will never use and which will quickly break after rounding off any tight fittings you encounter, taking the skin off your knuckles at the same time.

WORKSHOP SAFETY

Restoring any vehicle, even a relatively small one like a Vespa scooter, will throw up potentially dangerous situations during the process. Do not rush, take time to assess the task in hand, and visualise any potential hazards that may result. Read any literature supplied with power tools before use, mains electricity is a killer so a circuit breaker is essential. Fuel should be drained before work begins, and stored in sealed containers designed for the purpose. At least one fire extinguisher should be on hand at all times. Welding and grinding can send sparks over a considerable distance, so make sure there are no flammable materials in range. Always leave half an hour at the end of each work session to clear up and put the tools away; this will allow time for anything that might be quietly smouldering to show up before you call it a day. Protect your eyes and lungs from dust and fumes and be aware that old brake linings could contain asbestos. Wear appropriate clothing for the task in hand – thick cotton is the best material for overalls – and wear stout boots. Use a barrier cream on your hands before starting, and a dedicated hand cleaner with a moisturising agent afterwards. Remember to protect the environment as well, dispose of old oil, waste metal, plastics, etc, at your local recycling site.

DISCLAIMER

It is the responsibility of anyone undertaking work on their scooter to ensure that they are competent to do so, are aware of the risks, and have taken sensible precautions to protect their own health and safety. The author, publisher and retailer cannot accept any liability for personal injury, financial loss, or mechanical damage as a result of any information included or omitted from this volume.

THANKS

At times in any restoration a helping hand is required to deal with a stubborn fixing or to provide a second opinion as to whether the final body preparation is really up to scratch. My thanks must go to my mate Tony once again, for his assistance at virtually every stage of the process.

Chapter 1
Power unit

BEFORE STARTING

The Vespa Smallframe is fairly straightforward to strip and reassemble, but, to make life easier, arm yourself with a pen and paper so you can make notes during disassembly, and take lots of photos with a digital camera. What may seem obvious as you tear the motor apart may be a puzzle later once the memory has faded. Placing sub-assemblies into separate labelled boxes or bags helps, too. Inspect each component as you go, and make a shopping list of any parts that need to be replaced; it may slow things down but will save time and money in the long run. An engine stand is not necessary but makes life a bit easier.

REMOVING THE ENGINE

Getting the motor out is straightforward. Remove the engine-side door, and then drain the oil to prevent any unwanted spillage later (an old takeaway foil container is about the right size for draining into). Disconnect the carb securing clamp

The oil drain plug is helpfully marked 'OLIO,' so it cannot be missed. Dispose of the old oil at your local recycling centre.

Undo the screw on the electrical junction box and split the wiring, it may have screw- or push-in connectors depending on the age of the scooter.

Cable removal is straightforward: a trunnion for the clutch (yellow arrow), two more for the gearchange (white arrows), and a nut for the back brake cable (blue arrow).

(8mm spanner or socket), access to which is from inside the frame, after you've lifted out the plastic storage box. It may be easier to remove the fuel tank to give yourself extra room. The carb can be left in the frame for the moment. Undo the electrical connections at the junction box mounted on the swinging arm. Take a note of the wiring (it should be colour coded but often isn't). Free the rear brake cable (11mm spanner) and gear cable trunnions (usually

The clamp holding the carb is close to the frame (yellow arrow), the cable trunnion is accessible by opening the throttle lever (right-hand white arrow). Once undone, the cable outer can be pulled from its locating hole (left-hand white arrow). If it proves difficult to get at the cable connections wait until the carb is off the inlet stub, as this will allow better access.

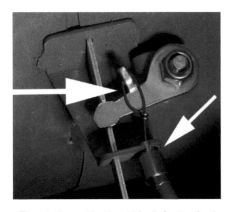

The choke cable should be left attached to the carb for the moment. Remove it from the frame bracket by pulling back the outer cable (right-hand arrow), and once out of its hole unhook the inner cable loop from the operating lever.

7mm, although sometimes 8mm if aftermarket versions are fitted), using another 8mm spanner to hold the main body body of the trunnion as you undo the securing bolt. Access to these can be awkward, so, to make it easier, remove the rear wheel (having first propped up the back of the scooter). Remove the rear shock absorber bolt at the back (14mm spanner x2). The main pivot bolt can be removed last (17mm spanner on

the securing nut). The bolt can then be pulled out, but it may well be stiff, so grip the head with a pair of locking pliers for additional purchase when pulling it out of the frame. Taking the weight off the bolt (by lifting the engine with one hand while you pull on the bolt) may aid removal.

The entire power unit, complete with wheel (unless you removed the rim for better access earlier in the process) and exhaust can then be dropped out, although lifting the frame up and away at the same time may be useful.

When the engine's out, remove any loose debris or heavy oil deposits which may cause problems later if you're not going to do a complete strip down.

EXHAUST/COOLING SHROUD REMOVAL

Before the top end can be stripped the exhaust has to be removed. This is attached to a cast elbow at the cylinder end by two 10mm nuts, and at the swinging arm casting by a single 17mm bolt. With the exhaust off, remove the cooling shroud (may be metal or plastic depending on age). Check the mounting eyes through which the securing bolts go, they're often torn, and plastic versions go brittle with age and crack. If the eyes are damaged add a new shroud to the shopping list as they must be completely sound to do their job properly.

Once out and on the bench, the cooling shroud can be removed. It's held in place by set screws (arrowed) ...

... and there is another one on the other side, under the exhaust.

The exhaust is bolted to an alloy elbow. This one has been bodged over the years.

The bottom of the exhaust is bolted to the alloy swinging arm casting (crankcase half).

Once removed, the reason for the bodging became apparent; damage like this is common.

CYLINDER HEAD

On 125cc engines, the head is secured by four 11mm nuts which attach to studs passing through the barrel and into the cases. Smaller engines have four bolts that secure to threaded drillings in the barrel itself, which is in turn held to the crankcases by nuts threaded onto short studs which pass through a cast flange. Regardless of type, loosen each fitting a small amount in a diagonal sequence until the tension has been released, then remove them completely. This method will reduce the strain on the casting.

With the head removed, check the mating flange for any dark staining indicating a leak and possible warping. Use a non-metallic scraper to remove any carbon build-up, a toothbrush handle cut at a 45 degree angle works, then degrease the head completely. Check for cracks, especially around the sparkplug hole, and ensure the sparkplug thread is in one piece. If everything is okay and the head is to be reused, tape some 600 grit wet and dry to a flat surface, such as a piece

The cylinder head securing nuts should be undone in a diagonal sequence until the pressure has been fully released; this helps prevent distortion of the head.

of glass, lubricate with a little aerosol releasing oil, then move the head around (with the sealing surface down) in a random pattern for a minute or so, then check to make sure that there's

Carbon must be removed with a non-metal scraper to prevent damage to the alloy. A brass wire brush on an electric drill will get into parts the scraper cannot reach.

Checking that the mating surfaces are truly flat is straightforward.

The cast ring which mates to the barrel will come up with an even shine if everything is straight. Dark sections indicate unevenness.

an even matt finish. If sections are left untouched then the head isn't flat.

Replacement heads are available for most models, whether genuine Piaggio or from aftermarket Italian manufacturers.

BARREL

The cylinder should slide off once the fittings have been removed, although access to the nuts on the flywheel side on short-stud motors can be awkward. It's possible that the barrel may be stuck on long-stud versions due to corrosion. Pour oil down the stud holes and try again after leaving it to soak in for a short time. If that is unsuccessful, then removing the studs themselves may be the best solution. Thread two nuts onto the stud, lock them together then use the lower nut to unscrew the stud. If the piston is seized and preventing the barrel from coming off, try soaking it in diesel for a while then giving it a good tap with a hammer shaft.

This is a 125 engine with long studs. Smaller capacity motors are secured by nuts to shorter studs at the base of the cylinder.

This is actually a Polini barrel with a different to standard port layout, but, regardless of type, all barrels need to be checked for scoring or other damage.

As the barrel is removed, support the piston until it can be gently laid on to the studs to prevent ring damage. Remove the exhaust elbow (held by

Stud threads are often damaged. Replacements are inexpensive.

Old studs can be removed by locking together two nuts on the threads, and using the lower one to unscrew the rod from the case.

The exhaust manifold is attached to the barrel by two nuts and shake-proof washers.

11mm or 13mm nuts depending on engine size).

Check the cylinder for scoring. If the damage can be felt using a finger nail then there's a problem. Check for a wear lip towards the top of the barrel. This can also be detected using your finger, but make sure that any ridge is not just a build up of old carbon (a wipe round with abrasive paper should give a good indication).

The nut under the elbow bend may not come off before contacting the manifold, which in turn may be stuck to the stud thanks to dissimilar metal corrosion. A combination of lubricant and wiggling it from side-to-side should get it moving.

In extreme cases, though, it may be necessary to cut the alloy of the manifold to free it.

Check the threads once the manifold is off, and run a nut down them to make sure that they are okay.

Bores also wear oval, which can really only be checked by using an internal micrometer.

If there's any doubt, take the barrel along to a machine shop and let them check it out. Do not be tempted into buying oversize pistons until the barrel has been inspected,

as it may need taking out more than one oversize depending on the extent of the damage. Check which piston sizes are still available for your scooter. Make sure to get rid of any old oil or dirt before taking it to be checked; it will be appreciated and your bill will be less.

There will be a gasket under the barrel – remove and discard.

PISTON AND RINGS

The rings can be removed by gently spreading them at their open end until you're able to lift them away from the piston. If the engine is having a rebuild then replacement should be automatic. Clean the piston carefully without using anything too abrasive, and check for signs of damage. This will usually be in the form of scoring on the sides, a rough top surface from detonation or debris in the chamber at some time, or possibly deformed ring slots from overheating or seizure. Make sure that the ring locating pegs are still there and not loose. The piston size should be stamped on the crown.

The piston is secured by circlips; this type of aftermarket clip is a simple sprung-wire device.

Piaggio versions have two eyelets ...

... which require dedicated pliers to remove them, which can be fiddly. A screw-type plier allows greater control.

Check the gudgeon pin for ridging or blueing, and replace if either are present.

The base gasket should be paper. Pull it up the studs and discard.

The piston is held to the crank by the gudgeon pin which, in turn, is secured by a circlip on each side. These should have two eyes and require circlip pliers to compress and remove. The pin should then push out, but will require some effort. A dedicated tool is available but it's not really necessary: gently warm the piston with a hot air gun then, using

Under the gasket, you should find numbers stamped into each crankcase half; these should match. This engine, which has been modified over the years, hasn't got matching numbers, although it still ran fine. Small frames built in the first couple of years of production have smaller crankcase openings, and spare parts for these motors are getting harder to track down.

a suitably-sized drift, tap out the pin. The piston must be supported fully as this is done, or there is a risk of damaging the crank. The easiest way to do this on long stud motors is to temporarily refit the barrel, leaving the pin exposed: on the others it will have to be by hand; use a glove or a rag to protect yourself if you are using heat to encourage movement.

LITTLE END

On very early Smallframes the little end was a bush pressed into the conrod. This type should be checked for signs of wear, such as discolouration and grooving. Check, too, that the gudgeon pin is a tight

The little end just pushes out of the conrod. It's difficult to accurately assess wear as the rollers usually just become looser with time, so treat this bearing as an automatic replacement in any top end rebuild.

sliding fit, and not loose in the bush. Piston availability is restricted with this type of crank, as the later versions are not interchangeable, so an upgrade to a newer-type crank with a separate bearing is the best way forward.

If you already have a separate little end bearing, replace it as a matter of course: they're very cheap. Check the gudgeon pin for marks or damage, and replace if in doubt.

FLYWHEEL/STATOR REMOVAL

Remove the flywheel shroud (this is simply screwed in place). There should be a bung in the centre of the flywheel under which lies the 17mm securing nut. A flywheel securing tool is useful at this point, or the crank can be held by passing a bar through the little end eye, and supporting it on a couple of bits of wood to prevent damage to the cases. Once the securing nut is undone, remove the shake-proof washer underneath. If the inside of the flywheel is threaded, you'll need a removing tool to get the flywheel off. The main body of the removal tool screws into the flywheel, then a centre bolt is done up, forcing the whole lot off the crank taper.

To help you get the flywheel nut undone there's a special tool to hold the fins steady. However, if the top end is down, then a socket extension passed through the little end eye of the conrod will do the trick. Use a couple of bits of wood or thick folded cardboard to protect the cases where the extension touches.

The flywheel nut should be under a plastic push-on cover. This is actually a late PK-type flywheel as this engine has been converted to 12 volts at some time. Normally, a light alloy flywheel will be fitted.

With the nut removed (17mm socket) fully screw in the body of an extractor then tighten the centre bolt. As it tightens, the flywheel is pulled off its taper. If it's very tight and reluctant to move, give the bolt head a sharp tap with a hammer.

With the flywheel off the stator plate will be visible. It may have two or three coils fitted depending on the age of the scooter.

If the central bolt is fully done up but nothing moves, give it a couple of gentle taps to persuade the taper to release its grip. Once free there may still be some resistance felt, but this

There should be timing marks cast into the case and on the plate: make sure they're lined up. If there are none, make your own using a centre punch or by scribing a line. Paint will probably not survive the cleaning process later so is not a good idea.

The plate should be secured by three setscrews, although it's common to find a variety of fittings replacing the originals.

Always store the stator and flywheel together. Doing so prevents the magnets weakening, and stops unwanted metallic debris clinging to the surface.

is only the drag exerted by the stator magnets and is easily overcome.

If it's an early engine the flywheel may not have an internal thread. Instead, there will be a circlip, and once the centre nut is undone it starts to act on the circlip and pushes off the flywheel. These clips often break,

so a replacement will have to fitted before removal can take place. Don't be tempted into using a general puller on the flywheel as it will crack before the taper releases its grip. Some early Smallframes also had separate flywheel cooling fins bolted to a central boss. Removal, however, remains the same.

The Woodruff key on the crank should be removed now and checked for wear. This usually shows up as a step between the part that sits in the crank and the bit that slots into the flywheel. If there are any doubts about its condition replace it.

The stator is secured to the cases by machine screws. Remove them and wiggle the plate free, gently pulling the attached wiring away with it. This can be tricky as the wires and the grommets they pass through can be brittle, so be gentle.

REAR BRAKE ASSEMBLY
The rear wheel is secured by either four central bolts or four or five at the rim edge, depending on type. The rear hub can be removed by undoing the centre securing nut, having got rid of the split pin which passes through it. This nut can be very tight, though,

The rear brake drum, in this case a PK-type is fitted, may be secured by a single nut with a locking cage and split pin on later scooters. Earlier Smallframes had a castellated nut secured by a split pin. The 22mm nut will be tight, and needs a fairly thin walled socket to get on to it. Once undone, the drum pulls free ...

... and the rear brakes are then accessible.

If you have the solid rim-style wheels, with four securing bolts in the middle, the rear drum is held on by a small securing nut (arrowed).

In theory, undoing this nut will release the drum for removal. In reality, the steel inner flange sticks to the alloy of the drum, and both may have to be removed together, by undoing the hub nut and sliding the flange off its splines.

They can then be separated whilst off the engine, although the process may have to be fairly brutal to persuade them to part.

The shoes pivot on posts, and are attached by these spring clips. Carefully push them off with a screwdriver tip, but be careful once the pressure is released – they may launch themselves into a dark corner of the workshop. Use the brake lever to open the shoes and insert a screwdriver behind one shoe, and lever it carefully up and off. This is fairly awkward for the first shoe as you're fighting against the pressure of the return spring.

The backplate is held to the case by three nuts – a 13mm socket is needed to undo them.

and it may be wise to release it when the engine is still in the frame (have an assistant lock the back brake whilst you undo the nut). Each brake shoe pivots at one end on a post secured by a horseshoe clip. Remove this with care as it can launch itself across the workshop as the pressure is taken off.

Pressed into the back of the backplate is an oil seal – it simply levers out. Note its orientation, though, the spring side of this type of seal always faces the pressure or 'wet' side.

There should also be a paper gasket between the backplate and the case. Remove it and discard.

The brake operating lever pulls out of the backplate. Any resistance is simply the seals; keep pulling until it's free.

There may be no seal, one seal, or even two if a PK brake setup has been fitted.

CLUTCH

The clutch assembly is partly covered by the crankcase casting, so may require some manipulation before it pulls away cleanly.

The clutch cover is held on by six 10mm bolts. The one fitted to the bottom left is longer, which is fairly obvious as the cover casting is deeper here.

With the cover off, the clutch assembly is exposed. Remove and discard the old paper gasket.

The pressure plate is held by a wire clip. Position a thin pick or screwdriver through the larger of the holes, and pull the clip towards the centre of the plate, and then out from under the lip of the clutch assembly. Unless the centre of the plate is unmarked, a new one should always be fitted.

With the plate out of the way, peer into the recess behind it, and you should see the securing nut. It has a locking washer to stop it coming undone. Bend back the tab of the washer and remove the nut with a 17mm socket.

A special tool is needed to get the clutch off, but fortunately, like so many of these tools, it is inexpensive.

The body has an internal thread, and screws into the clutch. The centre bolt is then tightened to free the clutch from the taper.

The clutch assembly comes away from its basket as a complete unit. Remove the woodruff key if it has remained in the taper of the input shaft.

The basket remains in place until the cases are split.

SPLITTING THE CASES

The bolts securing the cases don't all fit in the same direction. Remove them in a logical circular pattern and lay them out so they can be replaced the same way, or, if you intend replacing them, write down the way they face for later reference. Engines fitted with one-piece flywheel bearings are harder to split, and may require the assistance of a soft-faced hammer, used gently on the upper part of the case. However, before resorting to this, double-check that all the fixings have actually been removed first. In some cases heat may have to be applied to the case around the flywheel bearing casting to let it come free.

The inlet manifold pipe should be secured by nuts on studs, this one has lost its stud and has had a bolt inserted instead (arrowed).

If the studs are damaged or worn they can be removed from the case using the double nut method already used for removing the cylinder studs.

On the underside of the engine the cable guide bracket can be removed, two nuts to undo, and then the kickstart lever bolt can be undone and the lever wiggled off the shaft.

The cases are held by nuts and bolts around the outside, they have shaped heads so only an 11mm spanner is needed to undo them.

There are also nuts on studs which pass through the cases inside the stator plate recess. The flywheel side oil seal can be removed now with a thin screwdriver, or left until later as it will come off with the case.

The cases should part relatively easily, don't be tempted to lever them on any of the joint faces if they are reluctant to separate. Instead, try tapping the flywheel casting of the left-hand case with a soft-faced hammer.

Once apart, all the major components should be inside the left-hand case. The input shaft (Xmas tree) is in place in this case, more commonly it remains stuck in the flywheel side case bearing.

INPUT SHAFT REMOVAL

Sometimes the bearing comes out of the case stuck on the end of the shaft, if that's the case then the bearing seat must be closely inspected for wear or damage when the crankcase is cleaned later.

The input shaft should just pull out of the case without undue effort.

To release the bearing, try gently working around the edge with a screwdriver blade. If it will not shift do not use force, use a split bearing puller to move it.

CRANKSHAFT REMOVAL

The drive cog on the crank is secured by a lock washer, bend over the tab and undo the nut. A soft coin can be used between the teeth of the cog and the clutch basket, to lock them together to get the nut undone. Alternatively, it could be loosened when the cases are still together earlier in the strip down.

The cog slides over a woodruff key for location. Remove the key once the cog is off. The clutch basket has a larger gap in its projecting sides to allow the cog to be removed, so may need rotating into the correct position to allow removal.

GEARBOX REMOVAL

The output shaft can be removed along with all the gears, or the cogs can be removed before the shaft, in this strip down the gears were removed first. They are held to the shaft by a circlip.

The circlip has to be expanded to remove it; use good-fitting pliers, though, as it will be tight.

Check the cogs for wear to the teeth, chipping, or signs of the hardening failing, which will show up as pitting to the machined surfaces. Make sure the taper where the clutch sits is not worn (this one is) and that the woodruff key slot is not deformed.

Support the crank and use a soft-faced hammer to tap it out; it should not be tight.

Underneath there is a shim; it just pulls free.

The cogs can now be pulled back off the shaft. As they come, thread a cable tie through them to keep them in the right order, and, more importantly, the correct orientation as they are not machined symmetrically.

With the gears removed the shaft will look like this.

Tap the output shaft through the cases from the outside. Once again, use a soft-faced hammer to prevent damage to the threaded end of the shaft. Only move the shaft a small amount to begin with.

As the shaft moves make sure that the gear selector pivots (arrowed) are free. The shaft can be wiggled away from them once it is out of the bearing.

Once out, the shaft will look like this. There will be another shim (lower arrow), and a bottom circlip (top arrow), but these can be dealt with later.

GEARCHANGE MECHANISM REMOVAL

The gearchange pulley on the underside is held by a pin drifted in place. Tap it out and wiggle the pulley free.

Undo the bolt on the top of the case. It has machined steps under the threads, which sit inside the main selector mechanism, so it's quite long.

With it removed, the main selector mechanism inside the case is free to move. Pull the lever out of the cast hole in the case (arrowed) first. It then has to be manoeuvred to allow the shaft that passes through the bottom of the case to be pulled free.

CLUTCH BASKET REMOVAL

The input shaft (a) is still in position here. It passes through the kickstart cog (b) and, once removed, the cog is left trapped by the kickstart quadrant. Turn this and the cog can be lifted away, along with the loose spring underneath (c). Note the dished washer (d).

The dished washer is also loose (left arrow), lift it away noting its orientation, the centre is higher than the rim, then undo the circlip (right arrow). The circlip is an external type.

Once out it looks like this, the cush drive springs can be seen clearly; they will be addressed later.

REMOVING BEARINGS FROM THE CASES

Solid bearing removal is shown in the picture sequence. If your motor has a split flywheel bearing the outer track will remain in place in the case half. Heat the case around the track and then tap it sharply down on to a workbench, the shock should get it moving. If that fails weld two tacks on opposite sides of the track and then let it cool, the shrinkage should allow the bearing to drop out. If all else fails, then a carefully-aimed punch on the welds from the other side should drive it out.

The primary gear (clutch) basket can then be tapped through the bearing; once again a soft-faced hammer should be used.

KICKSTART ASSEMBLY REMOVAL

The kickstart spring can be released from the shaft with a screwdriver. Remove the spring and pull the shaft and quadrant out of the case.

The drive-side crank seal can be prised from the case and discarded.

The basket has to be pulled straight out to get it free of the bearing, then tilted to remove it from under the crankcase casting, it may need a little wiggle to persuade it to come out.

The kickstart rubbers are usually worn, so pull them from their slots and replace.

The bearing is held in place by an internal type circlip: it will be tight.

On the other side the bearing is shielded by alloy castings, so removal is achieved by using a drift from the side shown.

Heat the alloy around the bearing, using a blow torch with a narrow tip or a hot air gun. Then, using a socket or drift on the inner race, knock the bearing out of the case.

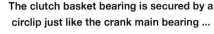

The clutch basket bearing is secured by a circlip just like the crank main bearing ...

... and it, too, just drifts out of a heated case.

The output shaft bearing on the flywheel side is a needle roller, usually like this but some early versions have no outer cage, and look more like a little end conrod bearing.

The input shaft is supported on the flywheel side by a small roller.

The best way to remove the two bearings is to heat the alloy case surrounding them, then tap the case sharply down onto a workbench. It may take a couple of attempts to get them out. If they are really stuck, putting the whole case in the oven and really cranking up the heat may be enough to allow them to be shocked free.

The small roller is often reluctant to come out. If the above method fails, peel back a small section of the outer cage with side cutting pliers, release the rollers, then grab a piece of the torn outer and pull the bearing remains out of the case.

The last remaining part still in the cases is the breather unit, which has spanner flats moulded in to unscrew it. Clean it in degreaser and blow through to check that it's not blocked.

CASE CLEANING

If you're looking for a concours finish get the cases professionally vapour blasted. If that's too expensive, then an alternative to scrubbing away at home is to drop them off at a local engineering shop with a professional degreasing cabinet. Ask them which day they change the fluid, and hand the cases over then. My local place charges less than the cost of a couple of sparkplugs for the service. Once thoroughly degreased, wash the cases thoroughly in hot soapy water to get rid of any residue. If the cases are stained give them a very light dusting with an aerosol case paint. Do not apply it very heavily or it tends to peel off when hot; just put on enough to cover any unsightly marks.

Inspect the cleaned cases carefully. The rotary pad may be scored, as here; this one is also chipped. If the damage is deep then replacement cases may be needed.

Finish off by cleaning the case mating surfaces with some fine abrasive paper to bring them back to an even shine.

The cases can then be thoroughly degreased. This can take some time, as old oil and dirt may cling to the many nooks and crannies in the castings, a screwdriver may be required to scrape out reluctant debris.

Check the bearing seats for signs that the bearing had been spinning, for scuff marks, or heat discolouration.

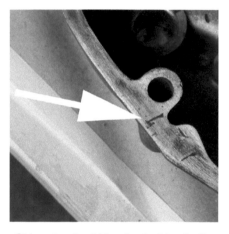

Old marks should be checked for depth. If the case has a lot, a jointing compound will have to used on reassembly, along with the standard paper gasket.

A domestic jet wash helps the process, but blow dry the cases immediately after washing.

Carefully scrape off any old gasket remains, making sure not to mark the surface as you do. If the old stuff is really caked on then aerosol gasket softener can help the process along.

The case locating stud will usually be rusty. Get it really clean and grease it.

REBUILD (GENERAL)

Rather than repeat the same suggestions in each section, there are some general guidelines which are good practice on any overhaul. Replace all gaskets automatically, paper versions can be brittle so dampen them slightly before use. Piaggio hasn't always recommended the use of gasket sealant, so grease all machined faces instead. All rubber seals should also be changed. All steel bolts passing through alloy should be cleaned and greased before refitting, to prevent corrosion build-up. Stainless steel bolts are not a good idea in alloy, as the dissimilar metal reaction can be rapid. All moving parts must be lubricated, so oil all bearings, cylinder walls, etc, as you go.

Items like Woodruff keys should be treated as automatic replacements, unless the originals are in absolutely perfect condition.

CRANKSHAFT INSPECTION

50cc Smallframes have a different crank from the rest of the series, with a 43mm stroke compared to 51mm. All have the 'small cone' crank as standard, which means 20mm bearing seat and a 19mm seal seat with an M10 flywheel securing nut.

New, high-quality replacement cranks are readily available in both sizes.

If your motor was fitted with a split flywheel bearing then the inner will probably have remained on the crank. It will not pull free by hand, so a split bearing puller will have to be used to drag it off.

On the flywheel side of the crank, check the threads (yellow arrow), the condition of the taper (double-headed arrow), the section where the bearing sat (inner arrow), and the seal seat (remaining arrow). Damage to any and it's time to consider a new crank.

The condition of the woodruff key slot is important, too. This one is badly worn, and unsuitable for re-use.

The drive-side of the crank needs to checked in exactly the same way as the flywheel side.

The big end can be checked by extending the conrod fully then carefully trying to push the rod in and out against the bearing, play here means a new crank, or at the very least the fitting of a rod kit by a machine shop.

The crank half that mates to the rotary pad in the case must be free from damage too. This one is lightly scored but not worth risking in a newly rebuilt motor so needs to be changed.

Split flywheel side main bearings make reassembling the motor easier.

When fitting the inner race, use a crank wedge (left arrow), opposite the big end bearing (right arrow).

When fitting, it has to be tapped down by the inner track. It should not require much force to get it down.

REFITTING BEARINGS TO CASES

Buy replacement bearings from a recognised supplier. There are lots of counterfeit bearings around (in packaging which is difficult to differentiate from genuine parts), most of which are sold via the internet at what appear to be attractive prices. New bearings have to be fitted by their outer track. Suitable drifts are available, but a close-fitting socket can do the job just as well. Bearings should be started off in their respective holes very carefully, to ensure that they're going in straight,

Buying your new bearings as a kit may be the most cost effective.

before you apply any force. If they go in even slightly crooked there's a risk of damaging the cases if you just hammer away, so take it slow. Localised heating of the cases will always help as well.

Solid flywheel bearings can be replaced with two-piece versions, and these will make future engine splits easier.

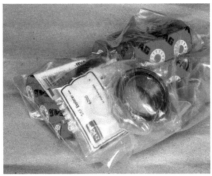

Wrap them in sealable plastic bags and pop them in the freezer the night before you're going to fit them.

Heat the case around each bearing seat in turn, and use a drift on the outer race of the bearing. As you tap them down, the note will change when the bearing hits its seat.

You can check progress by spinning the case over and seeing how close the bearing is to its seat.

Once seated, replace the circlips.

Check they are correctly located all the way round.

New seals can also be bought as a complete set.

If some help is needed, use a drift on the outer track and tap gently into place; excessive force here can crack the casings.

Heat the surrounding alloy as before, and use a good fitting drift on the outer race.

REFITTING GEARCHANGE MECHANISM

Once the drive-side bearing is in place, the new crank seal can be pressed in by hand. The spring side always faces towards the pressure source.

The needle bearing is delicate, it should be fitted with the writing visible as that side will be stronger than the plain side so will handle being tapped into place better.

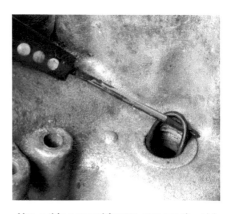

Use a thin screwdriver to remove the old kickstart rubber seal from the case.

The two blind bearings require most care when fitting. Make sure that the case is very well heated in preparation. If it is, the frozen bearing should virtually drop all the way in unassisted.

The output shaft bearing is fitted from the outside of the cases. Some wood underneath may help absorb some of the impact as it can be tight going in.

Oil or grease the replacement, and use a finger to roll it into the casting and locate in its groove.

The gear selector mechanism main shaft also has an oil seal which must be replaced before refitting. This is a common leak point on these motors, and oversized seals are available to compensate for wear.

Check the pivoting blocks for ridging. They are held in place by small E-clips. Leaving worn ones in place will compromise gearchange quality.

Make sure that the shaft is clean, free from burrs, and oiled before dropping it back into the case.

Swing the fork around, and insert the small locating stub into its hole.

Align the top of the selector with the top securing bolt and screw it into place.

Align the cable cog with the shaft hole and re-insert the small securing pin.

CUSH DRIVE OVERHAUL/ REFITTING/KICKSTART MECHANISM REPLACEMENT

The repair kit to overhaul the cush drive assembly is not expensive, but some have closing plates which are too thin for the job and distort when the rivets are fully compressed. Carefully remove the old plates and compare them to the new, it may be better to re-use the originals.

The clutch basket incorporates a simple spring cush drive. The teeth should be checked for wear. If a replacement is required, or simply to check the ratios, mark one tooth with paint and count the number.

Do the same with the drive cog which was fitted to the crank. The two numbers give the primary drive ratio, which you will need to quote to parts suppliers.

The sides of the basket can become grooved. Minor wear can be dressed out with a file, heavy grooving means a new basket.

The springs sit inside the cog wheel, and are trapped between two metal plates which are riveted together. Even if they appear undamaged, the springs weaken with age and contribute to a harsh take-up of drive.

Drill or grind the heads of the rivets to get access to the springs, which can then be levered out with a screwdriver.

The remains can then be drilled out from the basket.

They can be very reluctant to move, though, and may require drifting out.

Retrieve the metal collars which act as spacers between the basket and cog.

The necessary parts for overhauling the cush drive can be bought as a kit.

The new springs are a tight fit. Insert one end then compress the spring with a pair of thin-nosed pilers. Once the edge is in, the remainder can be tapped down with a small hammer.

Fit both plates, trap the spacers once more between the cog and basket, and insert the rivets.

Support the back of one of the rivets with a solid metal object and mushroom its head just enough to trap the plate.

Do the same for the other three rivets before working your way around and fully tightening them all.

Once through, re-fit the circlip to hold the basket in place.

Slide new kickstart rubbers into place. There are two types depending on model/ year.

The clutch basket can then be jiggled back into position and inserted through the bearing.

Push the kickstart quadrant shaft through the case, then insert the straight spring end into the locating hole.

Fit the dished washer and spring to the clutch basket shaft.

It can be reluctant, so a gentle tap with the shaft of a hammer may be required to get it seated.

Then use needle-nosed pliers to turn and compress it enough to hook the end of the spring into the slot in the end cap (arrowed).

The kickstart cog is fitted next. Check for wear, which shows up as rounded edges to the teeth.

With the kickstart quadrant halfway through its arc, the cog can be slipped through and pushed against the spring on to the centre of the clutch basket shaft. Hold it there and turn the quadrant so it's fully up, which will trap the cog in place.

GEARBOX OVERHAUL/ CRUCIFORM/REFITTING

If the gearbox was worn and the scooter is a three-speed model, then an upgrade to four speeds may be desirable. Most parts suppliers can provide all that is required in kit form: a new input shaft, four cogs, and a suitable selector (cruciform). The parts are a direct replacement for the bits fitted as standard.

When the gearbox output shaft is built back up check the end float before refitting. This is done by slipping a pair of feeler gauges under the end circlip and measuring the gap, which should be 0.15mm to 0.4mm. Replacement spacer washers are available in 11 sizes to bring the end float within specification.

The gear selector design changed during Smallframe production, early three-speed motors used a two-arm cruciform, later upgraded to four. The version fitted to four-speed motors also has four arms, but is a different size. There are also two versions of this selector, depending on the age of the scooter. Before 1976 (approximately) the

assembly was 52mm high measured with it standing on the circular end. After that date, and usually fitted to 50 Specials and ET3 models, it was 50.5mm.

SIP Scootershop in Germany sells a pair of machined blocks to aid fitting the ball bearings, which might be worth investigating to make this tricky job easier.

The output shaft should be checked for wear where it passes through the bearing. This one is ridged and marked, and is borderline for re-use.

The shaft wears into ridges where each gear sits as well. If you can feel the wear with your fingers, then it's probably too worn for future long-term use.

To get the selector out, the bottom circlip and the washer underneath have to be removed.

The selector slides up and down the grooves in the shaft to lock each gear cog in place as it is selected. Once the clip has been removed, it's free to slide all the way off the shaft.

Cover the selector with a rag before pulling it off the shaft, though, as there are sprung-loaded ball bearings underneath it.

It will come off looking like this.

Re-fitting a selector is a major hassle. Start by sliding the selector onto the shaft, and tilt it slightly so one of the holes where the balls and spring sit is covered by a leg. Insert a ball followed by the spring like this.

Place the ball in the track and roll it over the spring as the leg is pulled back. You must ensure that the other side remains covered or the whole lot will fall out. The ball has to be compressed using a screwdriver until the leg can be popped back over it trapping the whole assembly. This is extremely tricky and frustrating, so expect to have to try it a few times before you succeed.

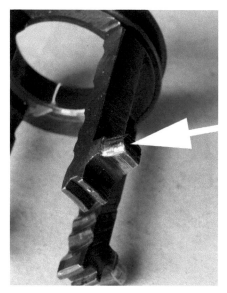

The main wear points are these lugs which act directly on the cutouts on each gear wheel. Unless absolutely perfect replace the selector automatically.

The other side will look like this, with the ball partially held by the leg.

Refit the circlip and washer to prevent the cruciform coming undone unexpectedly.

The spring and two balls sit inside the output shaft. These are released once the selector has been removed.

Compress the spring and trap it with the leg.

Degrease the gear cogs thoroughly, leaving them on the cable tie as you do so to keep them in order. Examine the edges of the four slots where the cruciform engages for wear; it shows up as rounded corners or chipping.

Inspect the gear teeth again for chipping or for signs of the case hardening wear which leaves pock marks in the surface.

Assuming everything is okay with the gears, slide them back onto the output shaft, and refit the washer and, finally, the circlip.

Insert two feeler gauges between the shim and gear cog face, and measure the free play. The gauge thickness must be the same on both sides, and a sliding fit with some resistance is what you're looking for. A range of different thickness shims are available to bring the gap within specification.

Fit a new seal to the brake backplate.

Add a little sealant around the raised casting which meets the case, and slide a paper gasket onto the the three case studs.

Change the seal on the brake operating arm, if fitted, and slide it into the backplate.

Bolt on the backplate. Alternatively, the backplate can be temporarily fitted to enable the output shaft to be driven through the bearing, and then removed again until the clutch cover has been replaced, as access is better with it out of the way; the choice is yours.

Guide the output shaft into the bearing, lining up the selector mechanism blocks with the cruciform groove (this is a little fiddly). It's easier if the cruciform is pulled away from the gears as far as possible to give the maximum space.

Once everything is in place, use a large socket on the solid metal of the back of the gear and tap the output shaft into the bearing. Don't apply force to the end of the output shaft, though, as it has to sit in the bearing in the flywheel half of the cases, so must remain in perfect condition.

REFITTING THE CRANK

Refit the crank through the drive-side bearing, it should push through with only moderate hand pressure.

Fit the drive cog, having first replaced the Woodruff key, followed by the lock washer then the nut, which can be tightened later, once the cases are secured.

REASSEMBLY OF CASES

Once the cases are secured, fit the flywheel oil seal over the crank and push it flush into its recess.

Grease the roller and needle bearings in the flywheel case.

Insert the input shaft into the bearing, the grease will help to hold it in place as the cases go together.

Grease the joint faces of both case halves, and put the paper gasket in place. If the machined faces were marked, use some gasket sealant (applied sparingly) to both cases.

The cases can be lined-up and pushed together. They often stick at around this point in the proceedings. Don't be tempted to use force. Instead, try moving the kickstart round and gently tapping the flywheel side with a soft-faced hammer. If there's still no movement, split them and try again, having moved the gear cogs around a little.

Grease the shafts of the case bolts and tighten them.

CLUTCH OVERHAUL

The standard clutch has three friction plates (corks), but it's not uncommon to find that the unit has been upgraded to a four-plate version, often in conjunction with an uprated central spring, although that's not really necessary for standard motors. Every part of a standard clutch is available at reasonable prices, so there's no need to tolerate anything in less-than-perfect condition. It's good practice to replace the metal plates as they can warp with time, so buy a kit with both included. The clutch plate tabs have to be aligned by hand whilst the clutch is compressed.

A compressing tool is needed to disassemble the clutch. If you don't own one, you can improvise using bolts, washers, and nuts.

Undo the compressing tool and remove it.

The spring and the clutch baseplate can then be separated.

Insert the tool and compress the centre of the clutch; this will release the pressure on the metal retaining ring (arrowed), which can then be gently prised from its groove.

Lift off the top metal plate with the chamfered edge.

The sides of the inner clutch basket wear, with the plates cutting grooves in the metal. Minor damage can be dressed with a file, but anything more serious will mean a new part is required.

The ring and the shaped centrepiece can be lifted free.

Lay the plates out in order. This unit had been converted to a four-friction-plate clutch; normally there are only three.

Check the metal tags on the plates, too, as they wear along with the basket sides.

Start rebuilding the clutch by fitting a new spring between the basket and bottom plate, and compressing with your chosen tool.

Make sure that the little tag on the lock washer is sitting in its groove, then tighten the nut and bend the washer over to secure it.

The clutch cover can the be bolted back in place. It's easier with the backplate off, as in this case. Always replace the paper gasket.

REAR HUB REASSEMBLY

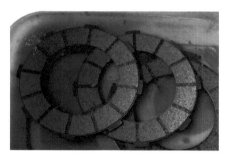

If you're fitting new plates soak them in gear oil overnight first. Fit the plates back in the same order they came off, followed by the top centre plate and the securing ring. The plates have to be aligned by hand so make sure everything lines up then release the compressing tool. Double-check that the securing ring is fully seated.

CLUTCH REFITTING

Remember to refit the clutch taper Woodruff key before fitting the assembly, which might take some careful jiggling to get the plates and the keyway lined up.

Refit the pressure plate, inserting the ends of the wire into the locating holes.

Drop the assembled clutch into the primary gear basket, fit the lock washer and screw on the nut. It may be easier to start the nut using a pair of long-nosed pliers as finger access is not great.

The brass pushrod (arrowed) can be removed by simply twisting the operating arm. Replacements are cheap. Grease the recess lightly before fitting the new one.

Refit the brake shoes by putting one shoe completely in place, and then put the hole in the other shoe over the top of the pin, and pull the shoe against spring pressure so it sits like this against the operating lever (arrowed), then tap it down into position. Put the brake drum back, followed by the washer and hub nut, which can be fully tightened later once the crank is locked.

FLYWHEEL REFITTING

Refit the stator plate, 12-volt conversion in this case, and align the ignition marks before tightening. The wiring is threaded through grommets to protect it; make sure they're fitted and are undamaged.

Refit the woodruff key in its slot.

Push the flywheel back on, having aligned its slot with the woodruff key.

Fit the shake-proof washer and the securing nut, and tighten. This picture shows a flywheel locking tool being used. If you don't have one, lock the crank as you did during disassembly, and tighten the nut along with the hub nut which was left loose earlier.

TOP END REASSEMBLY

Insert new rings into the cylinder, square them up and check the ring gap (should be 0.2-0.3mm). If the gap isn't large enough, gently file both ends of the ring until the gap is within specification.

The ends of the rings are notched to match the locating pins in the piston.

Double-check that the pins (arrowed) are there, and aren't loose. Make sure that the ring groves are completely free of old carbon if the original piston is being reused. An old broken ring is ideal for cleaning the grooves.

The rings may be quite loose, so mark the position of the locating pin so that, if the rings are inadvertently spun, it will be immediately obvious that the gap no longer matches the new mark.

To fit the rings, the ends should be carefully spread to allow them to be dropped into position.

Make sure that the gasket faces of the barrel are completely clean ...

... including the exhaust face.

The barrel will have a chamfered edge which makes fitting the piston much easier.

Lubricate the inside of the barrel well during assembly; engine oil or two-stroke oil will do the job.

Add a little instant gasket on the face of the cases, and fit the paper gasket. Oil and insert the little end bearing.

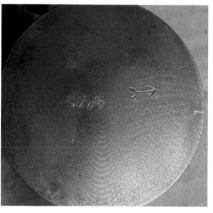

The arrow on the piston should point towards the exhaust port.

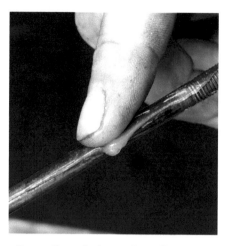

Grease the cylinder studs to discourage the build up of corrosion.

Compress each ring in turn, and insert the piston in to the barrel. This is easiest done before attaching the piston to the conrod.

Slide the barrel and piston down the studs together until the gudgeon pin lines up with the conrod, push the well oiled pin into the rod and fit the circlips. If the pin is very tight, warm the piston slightly then push into place with a gloved hand or a screwdriver.

Fit the cylinder head, the four nuts with their flat and spring washers, and torque to 12ft/lb. A low-range torque wrench will be needed for this.

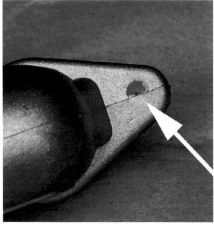

This new one came with partially blocked mounting holes. Run a file through and clean up any debris in the new castings.

The manifold bolts back in place with nuts and split washers.

REAR SHOCK ABSORBER MOUNT REPLACEMENT

Put an exhaust gasket in place ...

Tighten the manifold in place.

The rear shock absorber mount suffers from rotting rubber bushes.

... followed by the exhaust elbow.

The inlet manifold paper gasket should be treated to some gasket cement on both sides, as there must be no air leaks at this critical joint.

Screw a nut onto a long piece of threaded bar, pass it through a socket, which just fits over the rubber bush, then feed the bar through the shock mount. On the other side use a large socket which will sit on the alloy of the mounting away from the bush. Tighten the right-hand nut and the bush will be pulled out of the casting, and into the space inside the large socket.

The empty mount should be cleaned of all debris using abrasive paper.

Refitting is best done by inserting the rubber into the housing first, without the metal inner sleeve.

Then start the sleeve by hand.

The same threaded bar is then used with a large washer (arrowed), to prevent the rubber being pushed out at the back. As the nut is tightened, the metal inner is pushed into the rubber outer.

Minor adjustments to square things up can be made using sockets, etc, as spacers.

FRONT ENGINE MOUNT REPLACEMENT

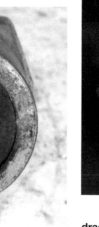

The main engine mount rubbers at the front can also sag with age.

If you look in the open section of the casting you should be able to see where the two tubes meet.

Using a screwdriver, it's usually possible to get one tube moving and out of the casting. Self-locking pliers can now be used to grab the tube to finally extract it.

The remaining tube will have to be dragged out, so threaded bar is used once more, with a nut on the metal tube inside the casting.

On the outside, a large socket gives the bush some space to move into as the nut is tightened.

Once it has started moving, the bush can be grabbed with self-locking pliers, and pulled out of the casting.

Once again, clean the inside of the casting thoroughly.

New mounts are inexpensive.

Lubricate them with a little soapy water, and start them in the casting with the help of a screwdriver.

They can then be pulled into position using the threaded bar and suitable washers.

The natural springiness of the rubber can work against you at this stage leaving a small amount of bush which is reluctant to go in.

If that's the case, swap over to a large socket, which fits as closely to the outside edge of the bush as possible. This will usually be enough to squeeze even the most recalcitrant bush into place.

In some cases the metal sleeve will pull away from the rubber outer, which will have to be levered out later.

Single-tube types may be completely stuck. Try drilling holes around the outside of the bush to loosen its grip before using a long threaded bar to pull out the metal tube.

REFITTING ENGINE

The engine can be slid into place then the front lifted and the main pivot pin inserted. The rear can then be raised and the rear shock attached. As the engine is lifted to do this, make sure that the inlet manifold pipe is feeding cleanly through its rubber doughnut in the frame. If a new pipe has been used the bend may not be perfect

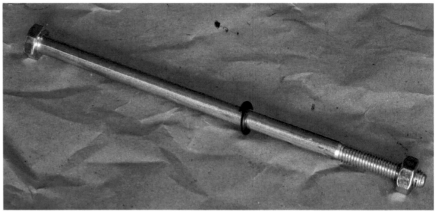

The main pivot bolt suffers from corrosion. If the old one is pitted it will not be long before rust gets a grip once more, so consider a replacement; they are inexpensive.

Support the rear of the scooter before trying to refit the engine.

The front gear cable at the headset goes to the left-hand side of the gear selector on the bottom of the engine as you look down on the scooter; this is why marking the cables is a good idea.

Replacement trunnions may have two 8mm faces rather than the original 7mm and 8mm.

and it may jam on the way through. If so, pull the rubber out of the frame back onto the pipe; it can be refitted from under the left side of the scooter later, using a screwdriver to feed it over the frame lip. With the engine unit secured in place the control cables can be attached. With the handlebar lever in neutral, slide the trunnions onto the gear cables, seat them in their cut-outs, and lightly tension the cable before tightening the securing bolts, making sure that the bar has not moved during the process. This will give a basic setting but readjustment will be required once the scooter is back in use to fine-tune their operation. The clutch lever will require some compression as the trunnion is secured to get the correct tension, so cable pliers are useful here. The brake cable will be too thick for the pliers in all probability, but it's easy to grasp and pull through whilst tightening the nut that clamps it. Wiring is simply a matter of following the colour coding, your original notes, or the supplied diagram if the loom has been changed.

STARTING UP

Refill the gearbox with SAE 30 oil, the filler hole also acts as a level indicator so overfill and allow the excess to dribble out for a short time before replacing the filler plug. Put a couple of litres of 2 per cent pre-mixed fuel into the tank – use mineral oil when running-in a newly rebuilt engine, as it helps things bed in better, swapping to semi-synthetic after 500 miles or so. There's no need to add extra oil, assuming that every internal part was well lubricated during the assembly process. Turn on the fuel

The gearbox should be filled with straight SAE 30 grade oil.

and check there are no leaks at any of the connections or out of the carb. Push the kickstart through its full arc

The best way of getting the oil in the motor is with a syringe: 20ml versions are the better choice in my opinion. Scooter shops tend to sell larger ones, around 50ml, which, although quicker to use, are a bit too large to manoeuvre around a Smallframe.

slowly a couple of times to prime the system, then turn on the ignition (if fitted), and kick over the engine to start. Expect some extra smoke as the internal oil burns off. Check that the engine is not leaking oil and that the exhaust is not blowing. Once the engine has warmed, adjust the carb as outlined in the fuel chapter.

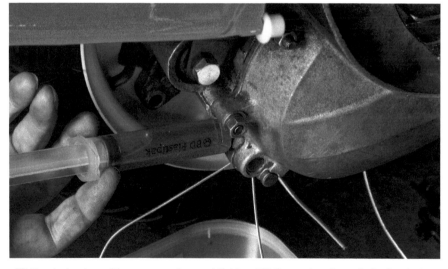

Fit the drain plug with a new washer and tighten. Fill the engine through the level plug hole. Deliberately overfill it, and allow the excess to dribble out before fitting the plug. Wipe the case afterwards.

Chapter 2
Fuel & exhaust

FUEL TANK

Fuel tanks fitted to all models are pretty much the same. The tank is held in place by 11mm bolts at the front, and by the seat post at the rear (assuming a dual seat is fitted). If there's a single saddle then a luggage frame will probably be fitted, and this has to come off, too. Once these bolts are undone, remove the fuel line from the carb, having first turned the main tap to 'off.' Plug the open tube with a suitable bolt. Turn the tap lever so it's pointing upwards, then lift up the tank at the rear until the lever comes free, which may take a little jiggling, then finally the whole lot will come away from the frame if lifted vertically.

The main problems with tanks are due to dirt and corrosion. If the rust is not too bad, there are products on the market to clean and seal the insides, but make sure that the one you buy is compatible with ethanol, as this is being added to fuel in ever increasing amounts. If the tank is badly affected by rust, however, new replacements are available, and,

Tank removal starts with taking out the plastic storage box. Squeeze the sides of the box inward, and lift it up and away. The tank is held by two bolts at the front, and the seat locating post (pin): all require an 11mm spanner to undo.

although they may not be absolutely identical, will do the job. At roughly the price of a couple of good quality tyres they're not too expensive, either.

Replace the fuel pipe and the securing clips during a restoration;

clear plastic versions are cheap and good for checking flow. If originality is important, then cotton braided hose is not much more expensive.

When refitting the tank, guide the lever back through its hole with your hand as you lower the tank front-first back into place. If you're struggling, a guide wire can be used to pull it through as you concentrate in lining up the tank to its frame aperture.

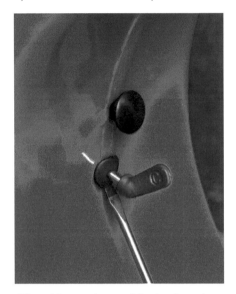

The rubber seal around the tap lever has to be removed. Push it into the frame cavity with a screwdriver, and fish it out later.

The filler cap is in two parts: the main flap which seals the aperture, and a locating knob which clamps the assembly down.

Expect to find signs of (mis)use. Here, for example, the original split pin has been replaced with a pop rivet, and the head of the knob is badly worn.

The main flap is held in place by a rivet which can only be removed once the peened head has been ground off. The remainder of the rivet shaft can then be tapped through the locating holes with a suitable drift. Replacing the rivet is tricky, though, as access for a hammer or drift to mushroom the head of the new one is limited. Consider a split pin of similar diameter instead.

All the parts can be bought new to renovate the assembly if required.

The main seal can be prised off with a slim pick or small screwdriver. It makes sense to replace this automatically, given the job it does; you don't want the tank contents weeping out onto any new, post-restoration paintwork.

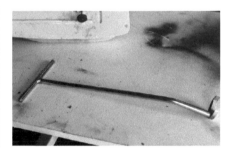

A special tool is needed to get the fuel tap unit out of the tank; it isn't very expensive.

The tap lever is held in place by an R-clip passing through a hole in the shaft. Pull the pin and it comes free. It's better to remove it now or there will always be the temptation to grab it when undoing the securing nut and it will end up bent.

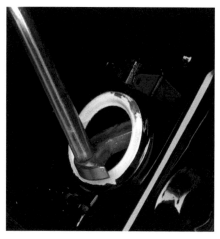

The tap tool initially appears too large to get in a Smallframe filler neck, but it will go if the larger side is inserted first and the rest pivoted in behind it.

Remove the wavy washer that sits underneath, followed by the casting which held the tap lever. Make sure the alloy is clean and free from any crusty corrosion which might damage a new seal.

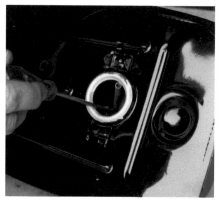

Holding the tap body, use a long thin screwdriver to start the nut on the threads. This is actually relatively easy as the threads are coarse and the nut can be wound on a long way before the special tool is needed.

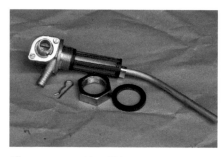

The tap assembly will look something like this once removed (although this is a new one).

The tap washer can now be removed using a slim pick, and replaced. Make sure that all those holes are completely free of debris. Locate the replacement securely and reassemble the tap.

Hold the tap body, making sure it's pointing in the right direction to allow the lever to pass through the frame hole later, and tighten the nut fully.

If the unit is in good condition it can be reused, but at the very least the internal seal should be changed. Start by removing these two screws to release the securing plate.

To replace the tap assembly insert it into the tank, remembering the rubber seal that fits between it and the bottom of the tank. Slip the securing nut over the copper tube and wiggle the tap to make it drop down to the threads.

The fuel line should be replaced automatically; it's inexpensive. If a full 'factory-fresh' restoration is being carried out, the the correct line with a cotton braided outer is available. The cheaper plastic lines may need warming with a hot air gun to soften the ends to allow it to push over the tap outlet more easily. Use a clip to secure the new pipe to the tap.

CARBURETTOR

Smallframes were fitted with flat-slide Dellorto SHB/SHBC carburettors – 19mm for 125s and 16mm for the rest. They all follow the same layout, with only minor variations.

The carb is held to the intake pipe by a clamp (and may have been removed already if the engine has been taken out). If you're only doing the carb, then loosen the clamp and wiggle the carb from side-to-side to get it free; this can be a patience-trying process. Be gentle and don't be tempted to use brute force as the mounting flanges can crack. Once off, unhook the choke cable from the operating lever tang, leaving it attached to the carb for the moment. The throttle cable can be released by unhooking it from the operating lever.

Cleanliness is essential when working on a carb, especially during reassembly. Parts can be cleaned in degreaser and rinsed in hot soapy water as long as everything is carefully blown through afterwards. Dedicated carb cleaner is better, fuel should be avoided as it contains many carcinogenic chemicals and is very flammable. If you don't have access to a compressor to supply the necessary air, pop down to your local computer shop for a can of compressed air (the type used for cleaning keyboards and other components).

If the scooter has been sitting for a very long time then it may have sticky internal deposits which are hard to shift by soaking and blowing through alone, if you suspect that may be the case consider having it cleaned ultrasonically, but price the total overhaul costs carefully, as a complete new carb is not very expensive.

The pictures here show only a strip down. Although something of a workshop manual cliche, reassembly truly is a reverse of the process. There are no hidden elements to worry about, and the carburettors really

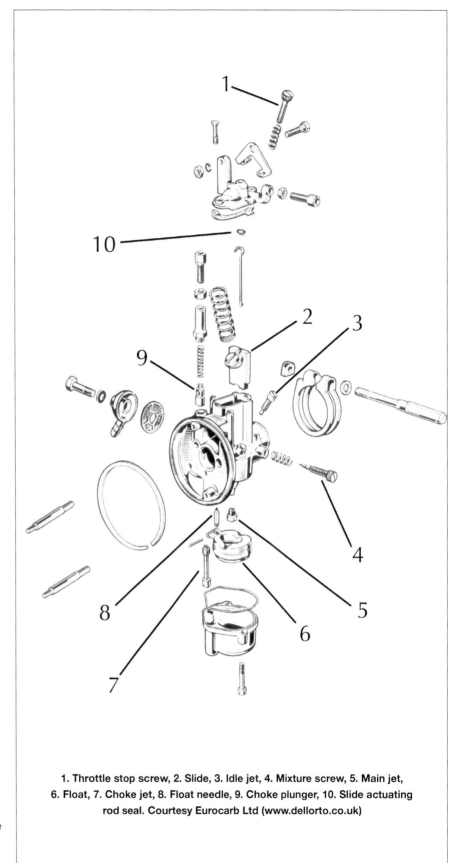

1. Throttle stop screw, 2. Slide, 3. Idle jet, 4. Mixture screw, 5. Main jet, 6. Float, 7. Choke jet, 8. Float needle, 9. Choke plunger, 10. Slide actuating rod seal. Courtesy Eurocarb Ltd (www.dellorto.co.uk)

are very basic. Bear in mind, though, that jets are delicate and shouldn't be overtightened. When replacing the carb, the outer cast alloy tube that the clamp sits over may push back towards the engine as you try and fit it. Hold the alloy from underneath the scooter until everything is in place. If a new rubber doughnut was fitted to the frame it, too, may be too generously proportioned to allow the carb to slip onto the manifold, and may need trimming slightly. Fitting a new throttle cable and trunnion is

(Cont'd page 51)

There should be anti-crush tubes inside the box where the carb mounting studs pass through to prevent any collapse as the securing nuts are tightened. If they're missing, replace them on reassembly.

The filter may be a top hat shape like this one, or a flat disc. Either way, gently pry it free and clean thoroughly. Replace it if there is damage to the mesh.

All Smallframe carbs are similar, and should look something like this once out of the frame. The carb is best removed with the air filter housing still attached.

The air filtration is very basic on most models, relying on oil-soaked mesh to trap dust and dirt. Thoroughly clean and degrease the whole assembly before re-oiling for maximum protection.

The choke cable passes through a threaded sleeve. There are flats machined into the sleeve to allow the use of a 9mm spanner to unwind it.

The air filter box is attached to the carb by nuts (indicated by the white arrows). These may be butterfly nuts on some scooters. The other nuts (yellow arrows), hold the air filter box together. Some late model versions will have a plastic air filter box.

The fuel intake filter sits under this cap, usually referred to as the banjo. A screwdriver or spanner can be used to remove it. Always replace the gasket on this fitting every time it is removed, and don't overtighten the screw on refitting.

Once the sleeve is undone, the whole choke assembly can be pulled out of the carb body.

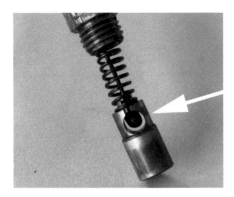

The cable can be released from the plunger by compressing the spring, which will then allow the ball end to be removed from the slot. Check the plunger for deep scoring or other damage, and make sure that it's clean; they can get gummed up.

As they undo the top will be forced away from the body under pressure from the slide return spring. Pull the whole mechanism carefully out of the carb body.

Once the spring is out of the way the rod just lifts out of the slide. Check the ball end for ridging or other signs of wear.

The cable-operating linkage sits on top of the carb and includes the throttle stop adjust screw (number 1 in the line diagram). There's no need to disturb any of this just yet.

Note how the spring sits in relation to the rod that pulls the slide up and down. There should also be a gasket fitted between the top and main body; most of it is missing in this instance.

The slide itself should be checked for wear where it moves in the body. Light marking is not uncommon but the edges should still be distinct and not too rounded, and there should be no grooving. If the slide is badly worn then the carb body itself may also have suffered. if that's the case then replacing the slide will not do any good; you'll have to replace the carb.

The top of the carb, including the linkage, is secured to the main body by two slot-headed screws.

To free the rod, the spring has to be compressed slightly to let it come away from its seat.

There's a rubber seal in the carb top which the slide rod passes through (arrowed).

The pivoting lever on top needs to be removed to get the rod out in order to replace the seal. Undo the 8mm nut and pull out the bolt. This will allow the rod to be lifted away.

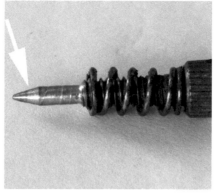

When the screw is out, check the taper for signs of wear, they often suffer from 'ridging' which prevents them working properly. Replacement is the only solution.

The float bowl is held by two slot-headed screws.

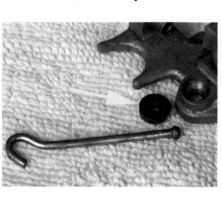

The ball will not want to pass through the seal as the rubber will almost certainly have hardened with age. Use pliers to grip the rod and pull it out. Getting the rod back through a new seal is much easier.

The idle jet sits next to the mixture screw and simply unscrews.

The rubber seal around the edge of the bowl should be replaced during the overhaul, although fitting a new one can be quite fiddly. This bowl is pretty clean. If the scooter hasn't been used for some time, expect to find sticky sludge – or even worse, solidified crystalline remains of old fuel – in the bowl.

The mixture screw (number 4 on the line diagram), has a spring around its base. Count the number of turns it takes to unscrew it completely, and reuse that number when it's time to replace it.

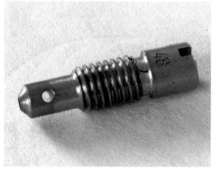

It will be stamped with a number, double-check it against the correct one listed in your workshop manual. If the jet is dirty, wash it in carb cleaner then blow through the drillings with compressed air.

With the float bowl off, the circular float itself can be seen (bottom white arrow). It's secured by a pin passing through two cast pillars (top white arrow). The choke jet (number 7 on the line diagram), is the top yellow arrow, and the main jet (number 5 in the diagram), is the other yellow arrow.

The float securing pin can be removed by pushing it through the alloy pillars with a suitably thin implement. The hole through which the pin passes can be clearly seen (yellow arrow). Remove the float carefully as the needle is slotted into it (blue arrows). It just pulls out once the float is free of the bowl.

If the pin sleeve is worn, the float can move around and contact the sides of the bowl, leaving scuff marks. Replacement of the float and pin is the only solution.

The needle tends to 'ridge,' and, as it's so small, it can be difficult assessing wear accurately. They're cheap, so just replace it, and upgrade at the same time to one that is compatible with unleaded fuel (these usually have red tips).

The main jet is also number-stamped. Check it's correct, then clean and blow through. Jets are also cheap and hard to assess for wear, so the cost of a new one could be very quickly recouped through better fuel consumption: consider automatic replacement.

The choke jet looks like this. Clean away any deposits and blow through just like you did with the others.

There should be a paper gasket between the carb and the air filter. Remove it and replace with a new one.

The air filter securing studs can be unscrewed from the body using pliers on the plain shanks; they shouldn't be very tight.

Clean the main body carefully and check it for damage. This often cracks around the mount to the manifold.

Blow through all the drillings with compressed air. Check and clean all the gasket faces ready for reassembly.

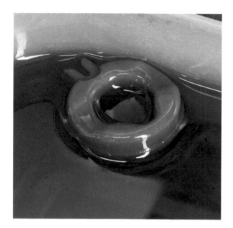

If you're reusing the old float, make sure that it's not holed. Let it bob about in some carb cleaner for a bit to make sure.

An alternative to a rebuild is to buy a new carb (luckily, there's something available to fit all models). This genuine Dellorto cost less than two tyres, so they're not expensive.

The carburettor clamps to an alloy sleeve which slides over the inlet manifold and is held by a wire clip.

The easiest way to separate the two is to push the clip around its groove with a screwdriver until the open end lines up with a slot, then pivot the sleeve to free it.

New sleeves are widely available (damage to the old one usually shows up as cracking around the slots).

Check them before fitting, though, as this one came with rather a lot of casting flash still in place. This can be removed with a file or trimmed with a sharp craft knife.

A felt ring fits between the manifold and the alloy sleeve. Always use a new one as they compress and degrade quickly. A light smear of grease on each side before fitting can aid sealing.

When the carb is ready to go back on it will slide over the inlet pipe attached to the engine (blue arrow), and is trapped between it and the alloy sleeve (yellow arrow). The whole lot is held tight by the clamp (white arrow). The felt ring is inserted before the carb is slid into place.

It ends up looking like this when in place (although the carb would obviously be complete, not just the body as shown here).

The manifold passes through a large rubber doughnut, which is held to the frame by this lip (arrowed). Have a look at the Frame chapter to see it in place.

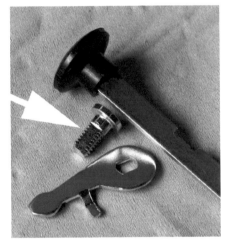

The choke mechanism is very simple. The rod with the choke knob passes through the frame, where it operates on a pressed plate secured to the frame by a special bolt (arrowed).

fiddly due to the restricted access afforded by the frame.

Once the overhauled carb is back on the scooter, it may need some fine-tuning. Use the throttle stop screw, number 1 in the diagram on page 45, to lift the idle speed so the scooter will not cut out. Then adjust the mixture screw from your initial setting and try and get the smoothest idle possible. Rev the engine a couple of times during the process and allow it to drop back to idle, as there is a natural tendency for

two strokes to 'gas up' if left ticking over for any length of time. Once happy that the engine is as smooth and even as it's going to get, drop the idle back down to normal using the stop screw once more.

Piaggio doesn't recommend E10 (ethanol at a 10 per cent mix) for engines built before 2000, so it's not suitable for a Smallframe.

EXHAUST PIPES

Exhausts suffer badly from rust as they're made from thin mild steel. If the scooter has been sitting unused for some time then they can also become blocked, as the old oily residue inside solidifies. If you intend reusing the original, then clean it internally by plugging the outlet pipe (traditionally done with a potato

The standard Smallframe exhaust is compact and very cheap to replace. Slightly less restrictive versions made by Sito, which look standard, may liberate a little more power, though with a corresponding rise in noise level.

Sportier Smallframes were fitted with a 'banana' exhaust. These are less restrictive, and are a simple upgrade for all models if originality is not an issue. There are a variety of makes on the market.

All exhaust types attach at the exhaust manifold/cylinder head and at the bottom to the swinging arm. 'Banana' types use a pin through a sleeve like this to allow them to pivot down to give access for wheel changes. Like many aftermarket parts, however, the fit may not be good. This pin wouldn't fit inside the sleeve, although both came from the same manufacturer!

Another common problem is poor pressing, which can result in misalignment like this. The only solution is to gently bend the downpipe until things can be persuaded to line up.

The exhaust system was not supplied with a gasket, and Piaggio parts books do not always show one fitted. As alignment may be an issue, it's probably a good idea to fit one to minimise the risk of leaks. The one fitted to the exhaust manifold at the cylinder head joint (8mm stud size, 52mm apart) should do the job.

pushed over the end of the pipe) and filling the whole system with a caustic soda solution and leaving it to soak overnight. Although effective, this is hazardous so read the instructions on the bottle carefully and follow them to the letter; the solution is volatile and a major health hazard. Gloves, goggles and good quality overalls are a minimum requirement.

External rust can be removed and the steel treated before applying a heat resistant paint as a top coat.

There's a choice of replacement systems, with a few genuine Piaggio exhausts still available, a range of reproduction standard exhausts, and custom sports types, but make sure that they are legal for your intended use, some are only designed for off road situations and are marked as such. Many aftermarket systems are a very poor fit, so expect to do some tweaking to get everything lined up correctly.

Chapter 3
Front end

HEADSET REMOVAL AND STRIP

The strip and rebuild is covered in the picture sequence. If the headset itself is damaged then replacements for most models can be bought, although stock can be irregular as they aren't fast-moving parts. New gear and throttle tubes are also available, but if secondhand ones are a more attractive proposition, then be careful as there are several different types, three- and four-speed, and they also come in varying lengths. The best solution is to take along the old one to compare against any potential purchase. Virtually all the fittings in the headset can be bought new if necessary, including guide plates, of which there are four types.

The headlight on very early Smallframes is not secured by the trim shown in the photos, it's simply recessed in the headset itself. If you're working on a model with a rectangular headlight, the unit is removed in the same way, but there's an additional support plate behind, which will have to be unscrewed and

removed as well. If there's an ignition switch fitted, it will be secured by an outer ring which will unscrew. There are usually only four connectors on the underside of the switch; note the wiring colours, and disconnect to remove the unit.

If new cables are being fitted then check how they fit into the

gear and throttle roller slots and ends before starting to assemble the headset. Even the better quality cables can be malformed, leaving the end barrel oval-shaped, which will stop them turning in their holes. Nylon-lined cables are the best option for smoother operation of controls.

All V-range Smallframes have cast alloy headsets. There are detail differences in some of the fittings, but the stripdown is pretty much the same for all of them.

The headlight can be removed first. It's usually held in place by the rim, which is clamped tight by a nut and bolt on the underside. With the nut loosened, the rim lifts off and the light will pull free. It may be necessary to loosen the adjuster nut on the underside of the headset, where fitted, to get the unit out.

The control cables can now be disconnected, but if a full restoration is being carried out then just take a note of how they all fit, and cut them once the headset has been lifted up off the forks. The same applies to the wiring if a new loom is going to be fitted. If you're reusing the wiring, disconnect the wires to the handlebar switch and feed them back into the headlight housing. On this scooter (Spanish), the speedo is held by a through bolt from the underside of the headset (arrowed). On most Smallframes there's a simpler bent metal bracket holding it place. Speedo cables are secured by a knurled nut which simply unscrews. The headset is held to the forks by a bolt which threads into a nut trapped in the alloy casting. A 14mm socket is needed to undo it. Once free of the nut pull it out completely.

The headlight should have a couple of locating tags on top (arrowed), so the bottom of the unit should be pulled forward and then dropped down slightly to release them from their locating slots. Disconnect the wiring to the bulb holder to remove the headlight completely, or unclip the holder and leave it dangling on the supply wires for now.

Don't waste time trying to prise off old grips. Use a craft knife to slice them down their full length, then peel off.

It's unlikely that the headset will want to lift off easily, so a few taps with a soft-faced hammer on the underside may be required to start it moving.

Brake and clutch levers are secured on the underside by a self-locking nut (8mm). The pin can then be unscrewed – it may be a slotted or crosshead screw.

On some models the underside of the headset had protection covers for the throttle and clutch control tubes, although these are often missing. Replacements in metal can be bought if absolute originality is required.

Use a screwdriver to lever off the switch cover, having centralised any controls in their operating slots to make sure that they don't snag. The main switch connector block is underneath, held to the headset by a single screw. Undo this screw and pull the block away from the bars, then cut or disconnect the wires as necessary. Take a note of the colour/connector number if the loom and switch are to be reused.

The gear and throttle tubes are two-piece, and are held together by clips (arrowed).

On some models the join is inside the headset rather than on the underside, the latter is shown here, but the principles are the same. The clip can be levered out with a screwdriver, but it can be a little fiddly.

The tubes can then be split, with the long section pulling out from the alloy casting. Watch out for this small friction ring on the throttle side.

Corrosion of the headset alloy, or a build-up of paint, as in this case, will often stop the tube from coming free. A combination of patient wiggling, some scraping, and a dose of lubricating oil will eventually sort it out. Gently heating the alloy where the tube passes through can also help.

On the gearchange side there will be a large metal thrust ring. It may be stuck to the headset with old grease. Put it to one side for cleaning later before reassembly.

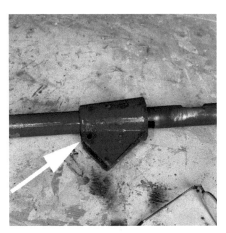

Check the tubes for ridging and corrosion, and make sure that the holes for the brake and clutch pivots haven't worn oval (arrowed).

Stripping off the old paint can be an illuminating experience. This scooter was originally orange, then blue, before finally being repainted red.

If the tubes are going to be reused they will almost certainly need a through degreasing. A cheap toothbrush is ideal for getting into some of the tighter spots.

It's surprising how much damage will be found during a restoration. This plate acts as the stop for the grips, and has been bent presumably from previous attempts at handlebar grip changes. It can be straightened with a combination of patience and a set of pliers. Light surface rust or pitting on the tubes will not prevent their reuse, but it's worth treating them with a rust killer and a thin coat of etch primer from an aerosol.

The gear and throttle ends can be cleaned with a soft wire brush, and the cable holes and slots checked for wear. The holes (arrowed) often wear oval ...

... as do the holes through which the securing clip passes, as can be seen here.

The clips themselves rust and the ends wear (arrowed).

The cable guide plate is not immune either. Some models have plastic versions of these, and must be checked carefully for stress-cracking.

If headset under-plates were fitted at any time, it's common to find sheared bolts in the alloy casting which will have to be removed. Grind the remains flush then centre punch them as a guide for drilling.

Choose a drill bit a couple of millimetres thinner than the shank of the stuck bolt. Try to keep the drill parallel to the bolt as you work.

A thin wall of the stuck bolt will be left behind which will give something for an extractor to get a grip on.

Heat the alloy around the remains of the bolt: it will expand more rapidly than the steel of the bolt.

Grease the throttle and gear ends, and relocate the washers in their correct holes, where appropriate.

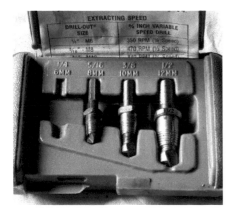

There are several types of stud extractor on the market, each with its own pros and cons. Screw in your chosen extractor and the bolt remains should, in theory, wind out with it.

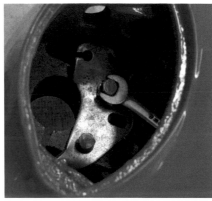

After painting, reassembly begins with by bolting the cable guide plate.

The threads can be double-checked by running a chaser or a tap down the holes.

Grease and reposition the thrust washer on the gear tube.

Remove any overspray from the holes through which the tubes pass, and grease them liberally to prevent any future build-up of corrosion.

Don't forget the friction plate on the throttle side.

With the tubes back in place, the headset needs to be mounted back onto the restored forks and the cables attached. This can be a three-handed job, so use a cable tie through the headset to allow it to be released as required during this process. Use a cloth to prevent the new paint getting scratched.

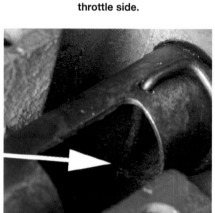

Line up the tubes with their ends and reinsert the clips. This can be tricky, so turn the tubes so you can see the bottom hole, and use a screwdriver to guide the clip end into the hole.

The wiring has to be fed through under the tubes and out through the switch hole. If there was a separate sub-loom for the headlight included with your new wiring, then it, too, has to be threaded into place. A guide wire can be used if it all seems too fiddly.

Mark one of your gearchange cables at both the headset and the gearbox end, as you'll need to know which is which when final connection is made or the gears won't select properly. Some cable sets come with different coloured sleeves for this purpose, in which case there's no need to mark them yourself.

The brake cable passes through two slots in the tube to line up with the lever casting.

Hooking the inners into place inside the headset requires some long-nosed pliers but they should all pop into their approximate places without too much difficulty.

The cables sit inside these 'top hats' where they pass through the guide plate and at the levers. New cable sets do not come with them fitted so the inner cables have to be removed, the top hats fitted, then the inners re-threaded; all of which is inconvenient and awkward.

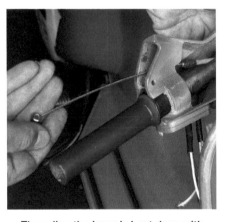

Threading the inner is best done with the top hat pulled back slightly from its seat; it makes threading the cable easier. Once started, the top hat can be pushed into place. If they are reluctant to go don't worry, they'll square up once some tension is put on the cable during adjustment.

When seated correctly you can see how the top hats centre the cable in the guides (arrowed). Once all the cables are installed the headset can be dropped into place, feeding the cables and wiring loom back into the frame as you do so. The securing bolt can then be fitted through the notch in the forks and into its nut. Align the headset with the mudguard so everything points in the right direction and tighten the bolt.

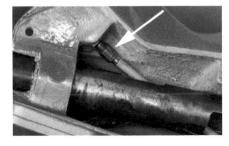

The seats in the headset where the top hats sit are small; don't try to get the top hats fully in place until the inners have been threaded through.

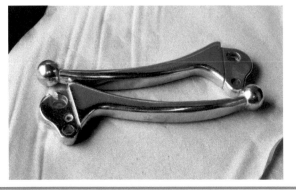

Old levers can be cleaned with a soft wire brush mounted on a bench grinder, then polished. If they're corroded badly and blistered, however, then replacements make sense as they are inexpensive.

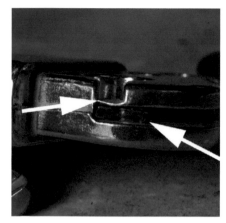

Inexpensive can also mean poorly made – these had casting flash in two places which had to be removed with a file before they were useable.

With the headset removed (this one has had all the cables and wiring cut as they were going to be replaced during the restoration), the forks will be clearly visible, as will the bearings and their securing rings (arrowed).

Don't forget the wavy washers which fit between the lever and the headset. Grease them, and the lever pivot points, before fitting. A small screwdriver will help to align everything before the pivot pins go in. These pins screw in and are secured by a new locknut.

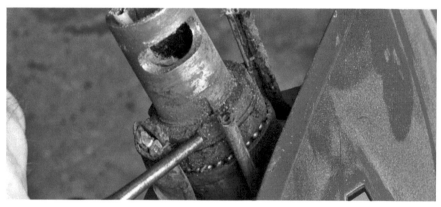

A C-spanner is the correct tool for removing the rings, but a drift does the job equally well, especially if nothing has moved in years.

STEERING HEAD BEARINGS

At the start of production, Smallframes were fitted with loose steering head bearings, although these models are now rare. Spanish versions kept them for many years after Italian production had swapped over to caged balls. Replacement balls can be bought, although the number of stockists is limited. The caged type bearings are shown in the photographs, but the earlier versions are changed in exactly the same way.

Loosen the top ring and remove it. There is a flat plate underneath, which simply lifts off, then a second ring which has the bearing track machined into it has to be unscrewed. Once this is undone, the forks can be removed from the frame and set to one side.

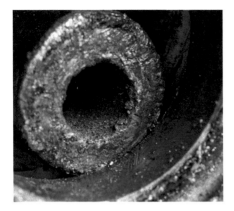

The top ball race will be left in the frame. Pass a drift up through the fork tube, locate it on the lip of the race, and tap it out ...

... it will come out like this.

The final bearing track and a dust cover are on the front forks. Use a slim chisel and insert it between the dust cover and the fork casting. Gently tap around the edge until the cover and the bearing track start to move up the leg. The chisel can then be used directly on the pair to remove them completely. There's a special tool available to carry out this job, but it's relatively expensive and, as long as you take your time, the method outlined here will get the track off without damage to the forks. Any minor marking can be dressed out with a file.

The bottom one is much harder to get out due to the frame construction not leaving much of a lip to get a drift on. Use a leg from a bearing puller, and jam it into position with something of the right size, in this case a chisel, then pass your drift down through the fork tube from the top and hit the end of the puller arm. This is awkward but does the job.

New bearings for the top and bottom can be bought as a set. They are inexpensive, so it's a false economy not to replace everything.

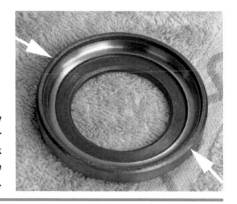

When fitting the track castings apply pressure to the edge (arrowed) only, never allow anything to touch or mark the track where the bearings run or they will be ruined.

A dedicated bearing driver is useful especially for the bottom track. A special tool is available for installing both bearings, it's relatively cheap but relies on a threaded rod to draw the tracks into place. Given that they can be very tight, it may not be effective in every case.

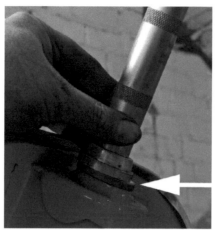

The top track is a piece of cake in comparison; again, make sure there's no paint where it will sit, and remember to grease the area.

There's now only a very narrow lip to work with, so a slim drift and a steady hand are required.

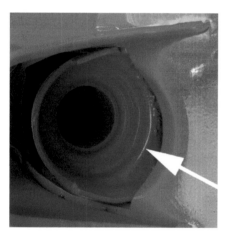

If the frame has been painted, rub down the area where the track sits, and apply a little grease to aid installation.

On the fork, clean the alloy where the track will sit, using some fine wet and dry, then slip on the dust cover; it will be a loose fit. Slide the track down the fork, and start it by hand on the edge of the alloy casting (left arrow); the dust cover (right arrow) will end up trapped against the fork by the race. Note that the mudguard has to be fitted first.

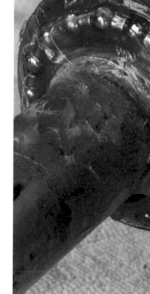

Fitting this track can be tough. Make sure the race starts off square to its seat, and be prepared to give it some hard taps to keep it moving. An assistant to steady the frame as you do this is pretty much essential. The sound of the hammer blows will change from a thud to a clearer ringing noise when the race is fully seated.

Tap the track down using the raised inner edge (arrowed). This is easy until the race is flush to the alloy, as shown here.

Once fully seated, grease well and drop the bearing race in place, then grease it too.

Refitting the forks is easiest with the scooter on its side. Slide them into place, making sure that the bottom bearing is sitting square in its track.

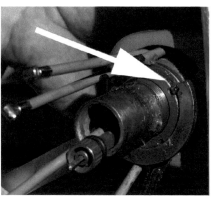

Fit the C-spanner to the slot and tighten the bottom ring. It's best to overtighten initially, to make sure everything is seated properly, then slacken off slightly before retightening so there's no free play, but equally no sign of binding as the forks are moved from lock to lock.

Up top, make sure that the track is well greased.

... followed by the slotted ring with the track machined in it. Grease this, too.

The flat washer comes next. Note the notch which mates with a slot in the forks. Grease the washer on both sides when fitting.

Slide on the bearing race ...

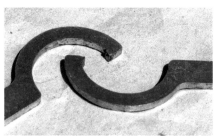

C-spanners are needed for reassembly. A drift can be used, but it's crude, and final adjustment is much harder. The spanners shown here were bought mail order, and were so soft that the operating surfaces were rounded off after using them for the first time.

The top ring can then be fitted. This acts as a locking ring, so make sure that it's tight.

And that's the forks secured to the frame once more. A final check on bearing play can be made once the scooter is back on its stand and before the headset is reattached.

FORK OVERHAUL

Brand new bare forks, which are Piaggio old stock, are currently available, as are all the fittings, so it would be possible to build up a completely new fork assembly if required. If fitting a new mudguard as part of the overhaul, check that it lines up properly with the forks before painting it. Misalignment of the bolt holes is not uncommon, and some work with a file might be needed to make it all sit properly. Some aftermarket guards come with a large enough hole so they can be slipped on after the bottom bearing track and dust seal have been fitted; check before assembling, if the hole is too small the guard will have to go on first, then the bearing.

All V-range forks are essentially the same. Very early models had smaller, simpler shock absorbers, but the layout remained the same.

The mudguard has a side screw which had been lost under a layer of filler in this case. It should be clearly visible.

The hub nut was very rusty, a common problem with scooters which have been neglected. Don't bother trying to remove the spilt pin when it is in this condition, just force a socket over the nut and use brute force to get it turning.

With the drum off, the shoes will be revealed. They pivot on a post, and are held in place by a horseshoe-shaped spring clip. Use a screwdriver to push it off, but be prepared for it to fly across the workshop when the tension is released.

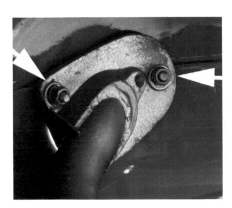

There is also a pair of bolts passing through the guard and the fork casting on top.

The braking surface of the drum suffers from neglect too, and pitting like this is perfectly possible. Professional skimming may be an option, but replacement is easier, and probably no more costly.

The shoes may be seized on the post, so use an aerosol lubricant, and work them from side-to-side, trying to lift them at the same time. Once off, the post can be cleaned with some fine wet and dry paper.

In this case the bolts were very rusty, so the mudguard was chopped off to allow better access to all the seized fittings.

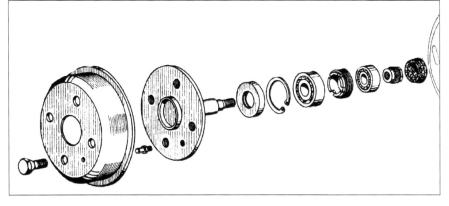

If your scooter has solid wheel rims, the drum slides over a guide pin. In theory, the drum should just pull off the hub. Unfortunately, if the scooter has been sitting, the drum will have seized onto the metal flange behind, and is often damaged when trying to remove it.

The operating cam is on a pin which pushes out through the backplate.

... lift them off and, underneath, will be rubber O-rings; remove these, too.

The whole hub can now be lifted off the forks.

Spin the forks over and remove the link cover, which is held by bent-over tabs on the rear. Straighten the tabs with a screwdriver and pull the cover away. Undo the two nuts which are now visible, and pull off the bottom half of the case.

In many cases though this may prove difficult as seized bushes steadfastly refuse to allow the shock absorber to pull away from the hub. If the shock is going to be replaced anyway then slice through the bottom eye with a cutting disc to release it. The brass sleeve may also be stuck on its locating pin, use self-locking pliers to grab it and twist repeatedly to free it.

Underneath, there will be a large and small washer ...

If it still resists, slice the bush too, just like the shock absorber eye, but take care not to mark the fork pin underneath.

The main speedo drive and hub spindle lives under a rubber cover which perishes badly with age; lever it out with a screwdriver.

The plastic speedo cog can be accessed by unscrewing this slotted cap. There is a sealing washer under the cap.

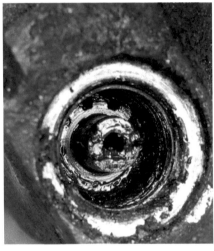

Once the cap is off, the cog can be seen, although it may be obscured by grease.

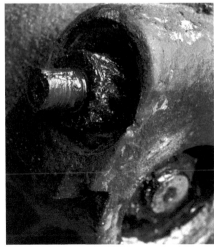

Use long-nosed pliers to grip the end and pull the cog free of the housing.

The main speedo drive, which was under the rubber bung, has a nut built into it, and the whole lot acts as the axle retaining nut; undo it (it's a left-hand thread) and remove.

The axle will come out with the bearing on the splined side still attached, but the retaining circlip has to be removed first.

Once the circlip is off, drive the axle out of the hub casting; it should move quite easily.

Once out, it will look like this.

Support the edges of the bearing on the jaws of a vice and tap down to release the axle.

Back at the hub, you'll have to peer into the recess where the bearing sat to spot the retaining ring which prevents the other bearing from being removed.

There's a special tool for this job, but an old deep socket with a piece of flat bar welded to it will do the job just as well.

The ring then unscrews (it has a left-hand thread).

With the ring out of the way the bearing will come out through here. Flip over the hub and drive out the bearing with a suitable drift.

Once out you may find it's metal-shielded, if original. Replacements will probably come fully sealed.

The final job is to remove the last of the rubber O-rings which sat on the bottom of the pins.

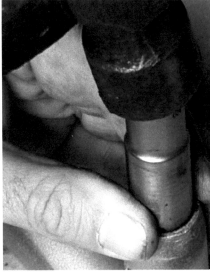

Clean out the inside of the fork and tap in the new bearings with a good fitting drift. If the bearings have a number stamped on the rim, drive them in from that side; it will be stronger.

The replacement bearings both came sealed, which makes for a cleaner installation.

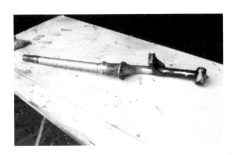

The forks are now completely bare. Check out the bearings at the bottom for damage or wear ...

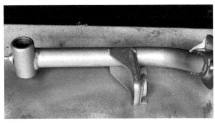

Make sure the grease nipple is clear, or replace it. Degrease and paint the fork legs: aerosol wheel silver isn't a bad match for the original colour.

Tap in the lower bearing first, using a suitable drift.

... they are thin-walled needle rollers and inexpensive. The old ones can be drifted out with a thin punch but they may collapse during the process.

Clean the hub and backplate, and give them a matching coat of paint, too.

Clean the locating ring thoroughly, and check that the threads are okay. This part was unavailable for a long time, but replacements are now being manufactured.

Tighten the locking ring, remembering that it's a left-hand thread.

Re-fit the circlip into its groove ...

A new rubber bung finishes it off nicely.

You can then either fit the axle – which should push through the bearing, although a light tap with a soft-faced hammer may help it on its way – or you can fit the bearing to the axle, and then fit both into the hub.

... then push in the oil seal which sits flush to the metal lip.

If there is the slightest doubt about the plastic speedo drive, change it.

Either way, when the bearing is going into its seat, it will need some help, so a deep socket used as a drift is a good idea. Put a liberal dollop of grease into the cavity between the bearings before driving the bearing into place.

Clean the axle nut/speedo drive combo, and screw it into place to secure the axle (grease thoroughly first).

Slide the drive into place, making sure the cable end is pointing in the right direction, then fit a new fibre washer ...

... followed by the screw-in plug.

The two pins on the hub have seals at the bottom. Those supplied were not a good fit, but, given their location, would probably be up to the job so were used.

Replacement shock absorbers made to original specifications are inexpensive. You can buy replacement springs, but the main damper cannot be disassembled to replace internal seals, so a new assembly is the only solution to a leaky or soft shock absorber assembly.

Grease the fork bearings ...

The hub pin was pushed through the fork bearings and another rubber seal added.

The top of the shock absorber is isolated from the mounting plate on the forks by a rubber bush on either side, always replace them when changing the unit.

... then fit the two rubber seals.

The shock absorber mounting pin was fitted with a seal: once again, a very poor fit.

With the top mount loosely pushed through its mounting plate, the bottom mount was slid onto its pin, followed by a rubber then a metal washer.

A metal washer is then fitted to the main hub pivot pin, too.

The upper mount top rubber bush was slid on next ...

The brake adjuster can be screwed back into place, having been cleaned and the threads checked for wear.

Replacement link covers are cheap, but may be of very poor quality. The bottom half of the cover is fitted over the pin threads ...

... followed by a large metal washer and securing nut.

The brake operating arm and securing plates should be cleaned, and checked for ridging or ovality in any of the holes. New items can be sourced easily.

... followed by spring washers, then the securing nuts, which have to be tightened.

With everything tight, the link cover can be pushed on and secured by bending over the little tabs on the side.

A little copper grease on the pivot is a good idea before it's slid into place. Some models have a rubber O-ring fitted here, replace it automatically when rebuilding.

New shoes are available, in standard or uprated guise. Don't be tempted by cheap versions as they are often poorly machined. Make sure that edge of the friction material has been chamfered, if not, file the edge yourself. It's a good idea to cover the braking surface with masking tape before fitting, that way the surface will not be contaminated by greasy hands.

Fit the bottom shoe on the pivot post first, then push the top into place against the operating cam. Put the second shoe on the pivot, then use a screwdriver to lever the top into place against spring pressure. Make sure your fingers are well clear, as the spring tension is considerable. Once in place, use a screwdriver to push the horseshoe clip onto the pivot post.

Replacement drums are widely available. Originals can always be skimmed to restore the braking surface if required, and the outside cleaned and painted using the same silver colour as the forks.

Split pins should never be reused, and a new castellated nut won't break the bank either. New hubcaps brighten things up, of course, and genuine Piaggio are the best (and not much more expensive than some copies, which are of such poor quality that they appear to have been made from recycled milk bottle tops).

New brake and speedo cables can be fitted to the forks using a guide wire taped to the new cable.

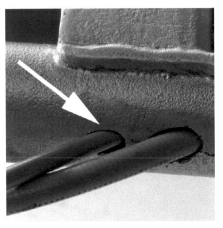

The holes in the fork are quite tight, so expect a reasonable amount of pulling to get the cables in place.

The speedo cable fits through the rubber bung which is secured by the metal plate and bolt. Make sure that the inner cable is properly located into its square locating hole in the drive before tightening everything.

Once the forks are refitted, brake cable adjustment is made much easier by investing in a pair of these dedicated pliers, it makes the whole job considerably less fiddly.

FOUR-STUD WHEEL CONVERSION

Many owners find the pressed steel four-bolt wheels unattractive, preferring the finned drum of the sportier Smallframes. If that's your preference, then, during the fork rebuild, the original axle with mounting plate can be ditched and the type shown in the picture sequence substituted. Bearings are the same, so the parts required to complete the swap are the axle itself, a finned brake drum and its securing nut and washer, a nut cover, and finally a new wheel rim.

Chapter 4
Frame

OVERVIEW

There are a couple of areas to note when restoring the frame. The Vespas in the initial production run up to 1967 were shorter than subsequent models, and some production plants made versions with slightly wider leg shields than the Italian models. Both these issues become relevant when ordering replacement panels, so check any dimensions given by suppliers against the original metalwork of your scooter. The other main change was to the size of the engine cover, which was much smaller until 1966, and was enlarged when the decision was taken to start producing bigger-engined variants.

Replacement panels vary in quality, with some being copies of Indian production parts for the PL170 models, and these may need minor modification to fit. They also appear to be made in batches, with the result that stock levels can be patchy. There is currently only one manufacturer of the small engine door panel; the part is high quality and the price reflects that.

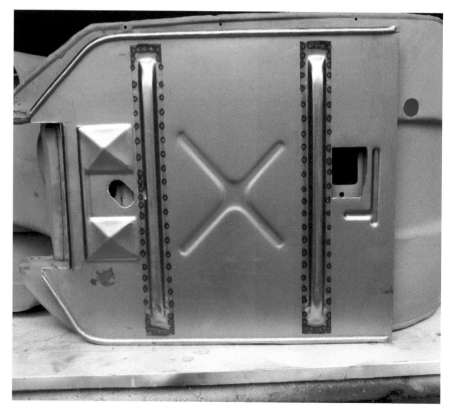

The Smallframe grew a few centimetres in 1967, and spacing of the holes for the wiring and brake pedal grew with it. Some replacement panels are poorly made, and may need quite extensive modification before they'll fit properly. Non Italian-manufactured scooters may also have wider leg shields.

PAINT REMOVAL & ASSESSMENT

With the frame stripped of all its parts the next step is to assess its true condition. If the scooter has spent its life in a warm dry climate then the worst you might find is bleached but sound paintwork. In that case sanding back to a level, solid base may be all that's required before starting the refinishing process. In most restorations, though, rust will have got a grip and the only safe thing to do to ensure its complete eradication is to get all the paint off and inspect the metal carefully. The best and most expensive method is to have the frame chemically dipped, often combined with a final electrophoretic coating. This process destroys rust and removes old paint in every nook and cranny, but double-check with whomever is doing the job that they are happy with the drainage on a scooter frame; they may want to drill a couple of extra holes.

A more commonly used method, probably thanks to it being much cheaper, is blasting, either sand which is cheap but fairly brutal, plastic or other softer media, which is a little more expensive, or soda, which is the gentlest of the lot. A local agricultural engineer sand blasted the frame in the picture sequence at around one tenth of the quote I got for dipping, so the savings can be immense. Make sure the operator has some experience of working with the metal thickness found on Vespa leg shields, though, or things might end up seriously wavy. The drawback with all types of blasting is that it cannot get into seams and box sections, and what looks like a clean, rust-free frame continues to harbour corrosion just waiting to eat its way back out once again. If a rough abrasive is being used, point out the location of the chassis number to the blaster and ask them not to linger in the area or the numbers may be damaged, or even removed.

Whichever method is chosen, if there's an option to have the metal primed immediately afterwards then take it, as bare steel will develop rust spotting within hours if left sitting in a damp climate. If the option is not available, then apply etch primer as soon as you get the frame back to your workshop.

If you choose to remove the old paint and rust yourself, there are a few options. If you have an angle grinder, then a twisted wire brush is really effective and can get into rust pitting pretty well. A slightly less aggressive option is a sponge pad which has abrasives glued onto it. These are flexible, and get paint off really well, but are less effective in removing heavy rusting. Paint stripper will also do the job, but it can be very slow especially on old, sun-baked surfaces. All these methods require lung, eye and skin protection.

With all of the mechanical components removed it's time to find out just how good the frame is. This one didn't look too bad in its thick coat of red paint; the reality was to prove rather different.

If you're going to have the frame blasted, degrease it thoroughly first and scrape off any old oily deposits and underseal or the blasting media will just stick to it.

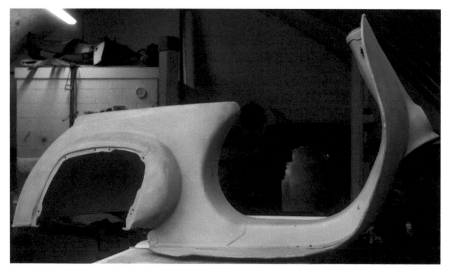

With the old paint gone it was pretty obvious that this scooter had some serious underlying problems.

Give the frame two good coats, but read the safety leaflet and the instructions on the tin before use, as the paint can contain some pretty unpleasant chemicals. Buy an appropriate mask and use it – you only get one pair of lungs.

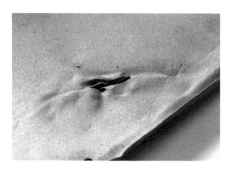

The floorboard was torn. Damage like this is hard to repair as the metal is stretched as well as distorted. If this were the only damage then cutting out the distorted steel and inserting a new section would be the best option. Cracking is also a common problem, but can be welded relatively easily.

Blow out the frame seams to remove any blasting residue, and dig out any bits of old muck and sealant which the blaster missed.

A wire brush on an angle grinder rips through old paint and rust, but it's a vicious method with lots of flying debris so take appropriate precautions.

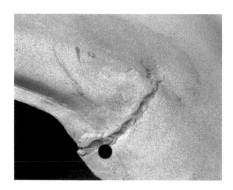

Previous repairs can be more of a problem if they've not been done well. This one, for example, has a suspiciously large gap between the two sides of the crack.

The steel needs to be protected immediately after getting it back to the workshop or rust will start to form very quickly. Etch primer is the best, either applied by paint gun, if you have one, or an aerosol spray.

Once the etch has dried the frame can be stored, handled, and worked on over time without worrying about corrosion getting a grip.

WELDING

Because Vespa frames are made from mild steel pressings, any repairs need to be welded. The best option for a DIY enthusiast is to use MIG. Small machines are relatively inexpensive, and a basic level of skill can be achieved quite quickly, although attending a course at your local adult education centre is highly recommended. Getting the work done by a professional is expensive and local options may be limited. If that is your choice, speak to your nearest Vespa club for recommendations.

FLOOR/LEG SHIELD REPLACEMENT

Leg shield replacement is shown in the pictures. If it's just a floorpan being replaced the basics are obviously the same, but make sure to measure the new pan carefully, then transfer those measurements to the old floor. Always cut on the safe side initially, and re-trim to suit once the new floor is clamped in place. Frame bracing should not really be necessary, but if you're in any doubt about the structural integrity of your scooter then run a short length of box

This is an Indian PL170 leg shield which is an adequate replacement for V-Series scooters. They are now hard to get a hold of, but pressings can be bought. They come without any of the reinforcing boxes and mouldings on the underside. This one was in storage at my local scooter shop for a long time and has a lot of surface rust; it was priced accordingly.

section steel between the headstock and the nose of the frame where the front seat mount is. The brace only needs to be tack welded in place. The replacement process shown is carried out from underneath the scooter. The reason for this is that it leaves the original factory spot-welds on the top of the central tunnel untouched, so, once the job is completed, the scooter still looks original.

The removal process begins with drilling out the spot-welds at the rear flange.

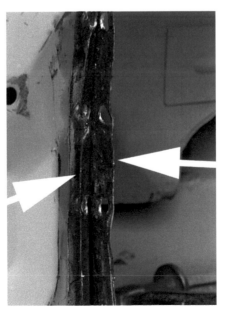

The floor is spot-welded to an upright on the rear frame. In this case someone had hammered the whole lot down against the floor after welding; the joint should stick out at right angles to the floor.

The reinforcing plates can be removed after drilling out their welds. This is only worth the effort if they are reusable; if not, don't waste your time. Replacements are available, and cheap.

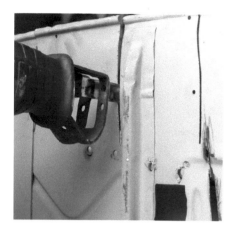

The floor can then be removed by cutting it down to and then along the join to the central tunnel. Cutting it in to small chunks make the job easier and reduces the stress on the frame.

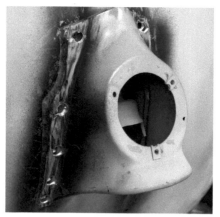

The old horn cast can be removed by drilling out the spot-welds. If it's rusted or damaged, new ones can be bought to suit many models.

At the top of the leg shields there is a strengthening bar to which they are spot-welded. Drill, grind or chisel to remove the old steel.

That will leave the section under the central tunnel to remove. Again, drill out the spot-welds from the underside, or grind the steel to weaken them then chisel off.

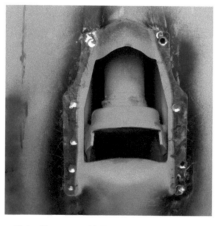

Note the rust which was trapped in the seam.

With the leg shields (or floor section if you are only doing that) removed, there is access to the inside of the central tunnel. Clean off all the old rust and treat it with an inhibitor followed by some zinc rich paint. Some of it will burn off when you are welding-in the new sections, but most will survive and protect the steel.

If you're only replacing the floor, carefully measure and cut. A plasma disc on an angle grinder makes an accurate slim cut, but be careful not to put any side loading on the disc, as they're very brittle and may shatter.

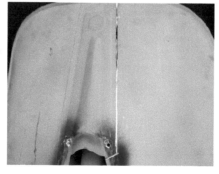

This upper horn cast was a pressed part of the leg shields. Complete replacements are on the market, as mentioned previously, but it was decided to re-use this section so a cut line was marked out initially. A thin plasma disc was then used once again to cut out the section.

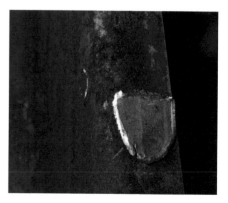

There will be quite a lot of other tidying up to do as well – these small metal tangs left over from the removal process will have to be ground off.

Clean the flanges back to bright metal. The visible tube is where the steering column passes through the frame; it's made from heavy gauge steel and just needs cleaning.

Carefully align the leg shields or floor section to the frame. Take your time doing this, and measure carefully side-to-side to ensure everything is correctly aligned. Clamp the repair sections in place with grips once the final position is thought to be correct, then check it all again. Once absolutely sure it's all correctly aligned, use a thick, soft pencil and draw along the central tunnel marking the new steel. Just as a double-check also make some marks at right angles to this on both the tunnel and the floor. Remove the repair section once more, and drill it ready for plug welding. The section which will end up covered by the central tunnel should be cleaned, de-rusted and painted, as this is the last time it will be seen; hopefully for some years. Make sure you don't obliterate your marks. If that's a concern, do this painting first before offering up and marking the new section.

The tube is secured to the central tunnel by hefty plates, spot-welded in place.

Clamp everything together, making absolutely sure that it is all exactly where it should be, and then begin plug welding. Move around the repair section randomly so that the heat doesn't build up in any one place.

Once finished, there will be a row of slightly raised bumps of new weld.

If you were only doing the floor, the front section has to be seam-welded across, including the section under the tunnel. This joint must be securely clamped during welding, and once again move from side-to-side, doing a short burst each time, to prevent heat build-up.

The horncast section rescued from the other leg shields was offered up and clamped in place. A new replacement section would be treated in the same manner.

There may be minor discrepancies due to the repair section pressing; the holes for the brake pedal, for instance, were not a perfect match in this case. Use a drill or file to open them up to get the correct alignment.

Do not expect everything to line up perfectly. This flange required some time with a light hammer before it followed the line of the new leg shields sufficiently well to consider starting welding.

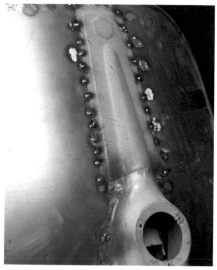

Whether you are using a new panel or a section from your old legshields as shown here, the repair will always need a skim of filler after welding to blend it in to the legshields.

BOX SECTIONS

These under-floor sections are very prone to rust, and, when they do, be prepared to find more rot underneath them once they've been removed. Replacements are readily available, but vary in quality, the cheaper ones can be much thinner steel than the originals. Always paint the inside of replacement sections like these, to help prevent rust forming in future, and consider sealing the edges as well. Wax injection after the frame has been painted will also be beneficial long-term.

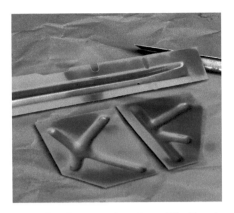

Just like the central section of the floor/ leg shields, the inner surface should be painted with zinc rich paint for future protection.

Plug welding is the best option ...

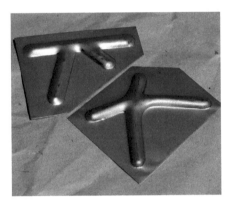

New 'X' and 'K' plates for the underside were purchased as they were inexpensive ...

The notch in the new section was lined up with brake pedal hole (upper arrow), and the cut-out kept parallel (lower arrow).

... it provides a neat finish and the panel edges are tight. Do consider using sealer on them after priming, though, and before the final paint coat, to seal them permanently.

... as were a pair of main floor struts. Like the leg shields they came with a fair amount of surface rust free of charge. Disappointing really, as they were new reproductions and hadn't been in storage for years. Note the orientation of the new struts, they should have holes or slots for the main stand return spring.

The new panels were all laid out to double-check positioning and fit.

Plug welding sections like these also affords the perfect opportunity to check that the welds are penetrating properly.

Once the welding is complete, the underside of the frame should be back to looking original.

HOLE FILLING/SPLITS

It's not uncommon to find that additional holes have been drilled in the frame over the years to mount accessories or racks. It may be that badge holes also need welding if the correct replacements cannot be sourced. If you're an inexperienced welder, clamp a piece of brass or a cupro-nickel coin to the underside of the hole to prevent the new weld dropping through. This will also help reduce the amount of grinding needed afterwards to get the surface level.

This box section is otherwise sound, but has a stress fracture at one end.

The final job is to grind all the welds flush for an invisible repair.

Small holes can simply be filled with weld. This badge hole was redundant.

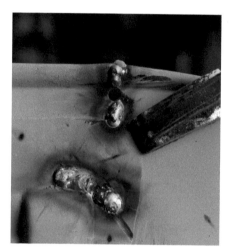

Repairs to cracks are simple: realign the metal carefully; clamp up and weld to secure.

Not all Smallframes have identical underfloor construction. This is a Spanish version. It has an additional plate under the rear box section, and only one rear strengthening plate. Reproduction of this setup is easily achieved at home if absolute originality is required.

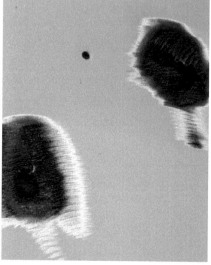

Once ground back the repairs will be invisible under primer and paint.

Careful grinding will produce an invisible repair.

OTHER REPAIRS

It may be that the frame is pretty sound but has a couple of small areas needing repair rather than wholesale replacement. Patch repairs should be done by cutting the damage back to sound metal, make the hole as square as possible. Using thin cardboard, make a template, transfer it to sheet steel of the same thickness as the frame section, and cut out. Tack the repair in place first, then finish by seam-welding.

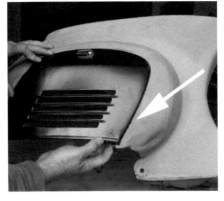

New panels should always be checked for fit before moving the frame on to the paint preparation stage. This engine cover doesn't fit the frame aperture, so investigation is required.

Access to get the hammer face on the edges of the dent was hindered by this reinforcing panel. It was removed by slicing through it with a cut-off tool. An alternative would have been to drill out the spot-welds securing it.

Holes mid-panel can be dealt with by cutting out the rot, keeping the section to be removed as straight-edged as possible. Make a template by drawing around the new hole on to a piece of cardboard held underneath, transfer the shape to fresh steel then butt weld it in place.

The culprit was a poorly executed weld we saw earlier, on page 76. The old repair was cut through, releasing the steel to be manipulated for a better fit.

The back of the dent was supported by a steel dolly whilst it was slowly beaten out with a panel hammer.

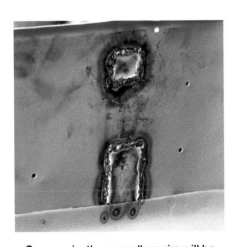

Once again, these small repairs will be invisible once ground down. A skim of filler may be required on very flat surfaces, such as the floorpan.

This dent was also affecting the panel fit, so it had to be dealt with at the same time.

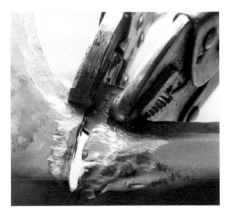

With the dent removed, the panel was pulled into the correct shape, which was double-checked once again by holding the new engine cover up to the frame aperture. The split was then welded up.

The floorpan pressing at the edge is often damaged and bent. A thick chisel can be used as a dolly, and the edge tapped with a hammer to get the rough shape back.

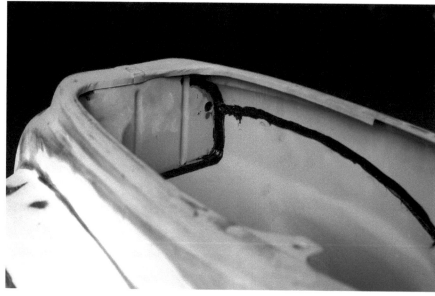

The shock absorber mounting area at the rear of the frame can suffer badly from corrosion thanks to a proliferation of seams. A repair section is available if repairs are necessary. Use sealant top and bottom to prevent water getting in and restarting the rusting process.

A drill bit of the correct diameter can then be matched to the floor profile.

Clamped in place it acts as a dolly, and so ripples and other imperfections can be lightly dressed away with a panel hammer.

DENT REMOVAL

Removing dents may initially seem daunting but, thanks to the single skin construction of the frame and panels, it's worth giving it a go. Always work back from the edge of the damage to the point of impact using a lot of light hammer taps rather than heavy blows. Support the metal on the underside, this would be done traditionally with a shaped metal dolly, but a block of wood will do. Try out the technique on a scrap panel first, an old mudguard or similar is ideal. Panel beating takes years to learn properly, but there's no reason why some basic straightening should not be possible, with any final imperfections being addressed during the filling stage.

RUST KILLING

There are dozens of formulations for sale for killing any rust which may be left in hidden corners or pitting on your Smallframe's metalwork. Long-term tests are regularly carried out by classic car magazines, so a little research should turn up more than enough information to make an informed decision. All products work best when the manufacturers' instructions are closely adhered to, so take the time to read them.

The prime candidate for harbouring rust long-term is the joint between the floor panel and the central tunnel. Get a wire brush into this gap, as deeply as possible, to shift old corrosion and debris, and treat the area liberally with your chosen rust killer.

CABLES

All the Smallframe models covered by this book rely on Bowden cables to operate controls. Simple and cheap they do suffer from corrosion, and wholesale replacement is sensible during the restoration process. Fitting new cables to a bare frame can be a pain, mainly due to the restriction in the tunnel from a reinforcing plate where the leg shields bend up towards the headstock. Many recommend passing a guide wire through the frame from the top, taping the new cable to it, then pulling it back out bringing the new cable with it. This undoubtedly works, but can be awkward and time-consuming. Instead, try feeding the cables down from the top as shown in the picture sequence, keeping them up against the leg shield as you do so. On most occasions they slide down relatively easily. Both methods benefit from greasing the outer cable leading edge to help it slip past the internal obstruction.

Replacement cables can also be too long. The correct way to deal with this is to cut the cable to the correct length and fit a new end. This should be done with dedicated pliers, sometimes referred to as 'parrot's beak,' but another option is to take the cable along to a local bicycle shop which should have all the right tools and parts (and is unlikely to charge very much for this straightforward job). If you decide to leave the cables over-length, they will still function but at the expense of some 'feel' at the controls. Cheaper cables may also have overly large ends which do not readily fit into the adjusting sleeves on the scooter, a careful combination of squeezing with pliers and a little filing will usually get them in place.

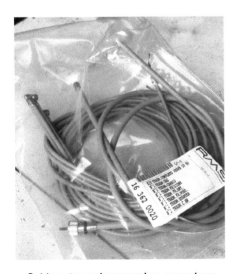

Cable sets are inexpensive, so replace them automatically during a rebuild. Nylon-lined versions cost more but last longer, and give the controls a smoother feel.

Feed the cables into the frame from the top.

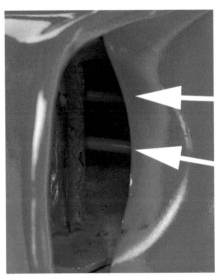

If you look behind the horncast you can see the cables progress down the frame.

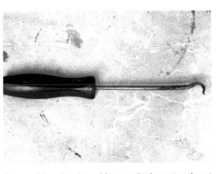

A small hooked tool is needed next; a bent piece of firm wire should do the job.

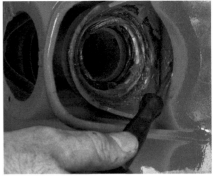

Hold each cable in turn against the leg shield with the hook. There's no need for a lot of pressure, the cable just needs to be held central and up against the metal; this will guide it through the hole in the frame pressing.

Once past the obstruction the cable will push through easily and probably poke out of the brake pedal aperture. There's another frame pressing to get through beyond that, but it's easy to guide the cable by hand from here.

At the back of the floor the cables exit through an oval slot which is sealed by a rubber plug like this. These plugs go hard and split, so replace it along with your new cables. Feed the cables through the rubber (and the wiring loom section which goes to the engine) before trying to seat the seal.

There's another rubber seal nearby, the doughnut through which the inlet manifold passes. It, too, should be an automatic renewal.

BRAKE PEDAL

A brake pedal strip down is shown in the pictures. Some late models may have a different version (PK type), which uses a cable with an eyelet rather than a clamp. Otherwise, the general layout is pretty similar. The cable clamp at the pedal has to be done up very tightly or it will release its grip under foot pressure. If the floor or leg shields have been replaced, do a trial fit of the pedal box and its bolts before painting the frame: the locating holes may need some adjustment using a round file to make everything sit flush once more. If the main pivot pin is badly corroded it may not be possible to drift it out for replacement. Fortunately, complete pedal assemblies can be sourced new.

The brake pedal assembly is held in the frame by a bolt into a captive nut (top arrow), and two bolts which pass through the floor from above secured by nuts (bottom arrows).

Once undone, and the pedal rubber removed, the whole lot can be wiggled free from the frame.

Undoing this nut releases tension on the plates which clamp the cable in place.

The clamping plates pivot on a rod secured with a split pin which is often very rusty. If it is, simply cut the ends flush with the rod to allow removal.

The rod itself is usually very badly corroded as well. The ends of the old split pin can be seen on the left-hand side. New parts are available.

The pedal return spring corrodes and distorts over time; replacements are cheap and readily available. The new spring can be hooked over the front pin, then pulled back into the locating hole using needle-nosed pliers; the tension isn't very high.

The brake light switch sits on a rubber seal, and is then secured by a single bolt (arrowed).

Once cleaned, replacement of the brake pedal assembly is the reverse of getting it out. There's a hard nylon bush which sits on the pedal and protects the underside of the floor; replace it if it's split.

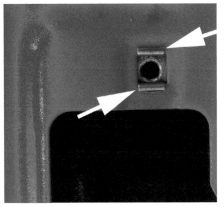

The captive nut in the floor also corrodes badly, so fit a new one. Push one of these tags into place, then use a screwdriver to compress the other against the nut until it passes over the floor lip.

When refitting the cable, pass it through the hole (arrowed) then clamp it between the plates (they squeeze together as the nut is tightened).

STEERING LOCK REPLACEMENT

One of the most common pieces missing from old scooters are the steering lock keys. Removal of the old lock is straightforward, but can be frustratingly slow as the last locating tumbler is deep in the barrel.

Replacing the steering lock starts by knocking off the flap covering the assembly. Bend the flap then tap it off with a hammer.

The securing stud should pull out with the flap; if not, then it will need to drilled out, which is a pain.

The lock itself has to be drilled out. Start with a drill bit around the size of the key slot (10mm or so). This should be enough to drill out the centre and release the lock.

Once the centre has been drilled out, insert a screwdriver, twist it to get purchase on the remains of the lock, then pull out the assembly. There will be a spring under the barrel (not fitted on Spanish models); fish it out of the frame, if it isn't attached to the lock.

Steering locks are not all the same. This section may be 4mm or 6mm wide, and the length may also be different. Spanish versions are not the same as Italian models either, so take care when ordering a replacement.

New parts are available for all models, though, and are very cheap.

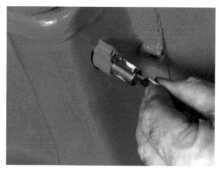

Clean out the recess in the frame ready for the new lock. Lubricate the barrel with a little grease, and slide it in, along with the spring if one was fitted. As you insert the barrel the key will have to be turned to the left to allow the securing pin to line up. Once it is, the whole assembly will push into the frame. Remove the key and the lock is in place.

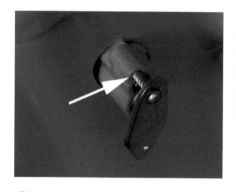

The new rivet for the flap is spiralled and slightly oversized for the hole. This is deliberate as it relies on an interference fit to secure it.

Use a small hammer to tap the rivet into its hole. As it nears the end of its travel, the tension on the flap is controlled by how far in the rivet is hammered, so check how loose the flap is as you go. It should be reasonably firm to turn or it will rattle around when the scooter is running.

SHOCK ABSORBER

The rear shock can be disassembled to remove the spring, but the insert cannot be repaired; so, if it's leaking, a new assembly is the only option. Springs can be sourced in a variety of strengths, and a heavier rider might want to choose a stronger version. The shock is screwed to a rubber isolating block which is, in turn, held to the frame by a nut and shake-proof washer. Genuine Piaggio blocks are worth the small amount extra as they last longer. Upgraded and sports shock absorbers are plentiful, but many carry a hefty price tag.

The rear shock absorber is separated from the frame by a large rubber buffer. Replace it, even if you're not changing the shock, as they distort over time and, if they fail on the road, the resulting movement can be extremely dangerous.

The thread on the rubber bush passes through the frame and is secured by a nut. Make sure that there is a locking split washer under the nut.

ENGINE COVER/GLOVE BOXES

These panels can be bought new and are relatively inexpensive so replacement rather than repair might make the most sense. The exception relates to the rare, early small engine door, which costs around four times more than the later, large version. Locking doors are available, and these obviously offer greater security.

Leg shield mounted boxes were fitted for some markets, and remanufactured versions can be used to replace damaged ones or used as a retro fitment if extra space is needed. Those models fitted with a small box in the rear side panel have the lids secured by a split pin, making removal straightforward. New lids and seals are available; as are locks, which are held in place by a simple forked metal plate. Use pliers and pull off the plate to free the assembly. Grease the new plate before fitting.

The engine side door pressing has rubber bungs inserted to prevent rattles. These can be bought individually or as a set. They are pulled into place from the rear using the tapered end, although some assistance from a screwdriver on the front to push the lip into place is also often required.

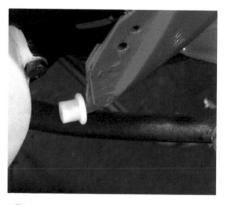

The door hinges on small nylon bushes, which are often missing or damaged. They simply push into place, although they may be tight.

Chapter 5
Paint

DECISION TIME

No matter how good the rest of your restoration efforts have been, most people are going to judge the whole project on its paintwork. Getting a good finish at home is perfectly possible, although it is unlikely to be show-stopping, so it may be the time to consider handing things over to a professional. If you do, have a look at their recent work on other scooters (or cars if it's a general bodyshop), and make sure that you get a written quotation. Ask them to include final finishing, which will ensure that any minor defects you have missed during the preparation stages will be their responsibility to find and rectify, although it will obviously cost more money.

COLOUR CHOICE

If a factory fresh restoration is your aim, then your local paint shop may be able to colour match from an unfaded part of the scooter, such as the inside of the glovebox lid. Piaggio codes, which can be found online quite easily, are generally Max Meyer numbers, and, although conversion charts to paint manufacturers such as PPG exist, sometimes the actual mixed colour loses a little in translation (or perhaps that was just the paint shop I used). Another option is to buy the rather expensive *Vespa Tecnica Volume 6,* which includes swatches for colour matching. Fiat car colours of the period are also often a good match for scooter colours. The final alternative is paint it in any colour that takes your fancy and forget originality!

PAINT CHOICE

DIY options are very limited here, as home use essentially means cellulose or enamel paints. The latter dries very slowly, so unless it's applied perfectly, defects cannot be addressed. Cellulose really is the best choice when it comes to doing the job yourself. Having made that decision, you'll need to find someone who can mix the particular shade you're after; or choose an off-the-shelf colour.

WHAT YOU NEED

Starting with the blindingly obvious, a spray gun. These vary greatly in price, but, unless you invest in a powerful compressor, buying anything other than the most basic of guns will be a waste of money. To be able to spray something even as small as a Vespa, you'll need a 2hp compressor with at least a 50-litre tank, along with a water trap and an air line, plus couplings. Budget compressors are nearly always direct drive, and tend to be very noisy in operation, so the neighbours are unlikely to be impressed, even if they don't notice the clouds of overspray that you are likely to create (so a workshop tucked well away from other people will be an advantage). Aside from plenty of space, good lighting is also essential when painting. Fluorescent strip lights are the most economical solution, but they really should be sealed to prevent the flammable paint cloud being accidentally ignited.

Moving on to personal requirements, the most important is a dedicated mask with replaceable filters suited to the paint type you'll be using. Clean overalls are a good

Painting at home is going to involve investing in a lot of equipment. Do not cut corners when it comes to protecting yourself, especially your lungs. A top quality mask suitable for use with cellulose paint will cost around the price of a new tyre, and is money very well spent.

idea, or even better a set of paper disposable ones with a hood, plus surgical gloves. Buy these from your paint shop as not all of them will resist thinners and solvents, and can rapidly dissolve into a gooey mess.

FILLER

Despite having a poor reputation thanks to misuse by the dodgier end of the motor trade, filler is an essential tool to the restorer. It's not designed to fill large dents, those should be beaten out first, but as a final thin skim to level surfaces it's a godsend. It needs to be mixed throughly to expel as much air before application as possible, and spread across the surface in long clean sweeps. Filler should really only be applied to bare metal which has been roughed up to give it a key, a blasted surface may be too smooth, for example. Modern formulations, though, will stick to pretty much any sanded surface, so there's no need to be too worried if a little etch is left behind as you prepare the surface. It should be left to dry overnight, as, although it may feel touch dry, it will continue to shrink for some time. It should initially be sanded back with a fairly rough paper to get some shape into the repair, then finished off with some 240 grade

or similar, which will also remove the flatting marks.

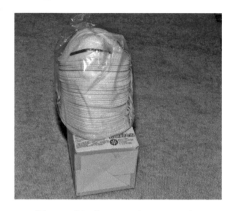

Disposable dust masks are useful during the sanding process, and are absolutely indispensable once you start sanding down filler. They are very cheap protection.

Dents and rippling to the steel should be visible even through the etch coat. Get back to the bare metal if you're going to use filler as it will not stick to paint. Using a flat sanding surface, like a dual-action sander, leaves paint in the depressions which makes them really stand out. It still needs to be removed, though, so a rotary wire brush on a drill or angle grinder is useful.

Depending on the extent of the damage it may be possible to just fill the imperfections and level it up to the original bodywork.

Don't buy cheap filler, it tends to be heavy making it hard to apply, and, once set, it feels more like concrete when you try to sand it back. Buy something labelled 'easy sand,' or words to that effect. Mix it thoroughly to minimise the chance of trapped air pockets developing, which would ruin the surface.

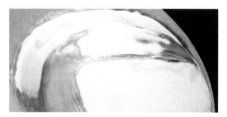

When there a lot of imperfections in the metalwork, it may be a lot simpler to use a light skim over the whole lot and create your own level. This generally gives a quicker and better finish if you're unused to bodywork preparation.

When a section has been let in, such as the horncast repair outlined in the Frame chapter, it will usually be necessary to extend the area covered by filler a lot further from the repair than you would initially imagine. Although these leg shields are new they still needed a lot of filler to lose the repair. The minor pressing in the shields was also lost at this stage, as it was decided a better finish could be achieved by extending the repair area beyond them.

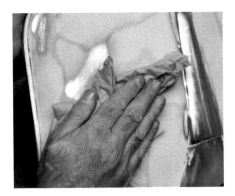

Before priming (or re-etching, depending on the amount of bare metal exposed during the filling process), make sure all the dust is wiped away, or subsequent coatings will not adhere properly. Your paint supplier will sell rolls of this blue paper designed for this use, but good quality non-printed kitchen towel could also be used.

WORKSHOP PREPARATION

Most home restorers are not going to have the luxury of a dedicated spray booth, so some basic steps will be needed to get the workshop ready. Cleanliness when painting is essential, and having gone through the filler stage there's likely to be a lot of dust about. Vacuum everything accessible then dampen the floor, blow off all accessible surfaces including rafters/roof supports, and leave it all for half an hour. Sweep out the shop and repeat the process. If possible, rig up some sort of tent above the scooter to prevent any more debris which might be lurking from dropping on the scooter during painting.

Double-check that there are no possible sources of ignition. Turn off and unplug all electrical appliances, apart from the compressor (obviously).

NEW PANELS

New panels may come in transport primer or bare metal oiled for protection. If the former, sand off as much of the primer as possible before etching and then priming it yourself. If the panel was oiled, degrease the

surface with panel wipe and paper cloth (changed frequently). Seams can be difficult to get the oil out of, so flush them well. Once clean, run a sander over the surface to rough it up slightly, then apply etch.

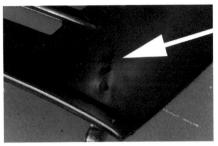

Just because a panel is new doesn't mean it will be defect free. Minor bumps in storage or transit are common. This engine door shows up another problem, the spot-welds holding the hinge flaps are prominent, so a decision will have to made as to how much they will show through the new paint, and whether it's worth filling the area to lose them.

Some panels come in bare metal, oiled for storage; this can be a real pain. Use copious amounts of panel wipe and lots of blue paper to wipe the surface clean, then etch and prime.

Replacement mudguards and the like will usually come in black transport primer. This primer adheres pretty well, but if the part has been stored for any length of time, corrosion can break out and creep under the surface, so it's good practice to sand back to bare metal. Once sanded, apply etch primer, then prepare the surface using the same techniques as were used for the frame.

MASKING UP

It makes sense to ensure that bolt holes and studs on the frame do not get full of paint, likewise bearing surfaces on forks or headstock races if they're not being replaced. Buy masking tape from your paint supplier, it will be better quality than the stuff from general DIY stores. No matter what it's being applied to, leave a small folded section at the end to make removal easier. Get the tape off before the paint fully hardens, or there is a risk that it will lift the paint during removal. It also tends to harden once exposed to the chemicals in the paint.

ETCH

Read the instructions on the can of etch primer carefully before use. All contain acid, and some contain other unpleasant chemicals, so follow the safety precautions to the letter.

Having done all the required repairs and filling, it's a good idea to re-etch the metalwork, so apply another couple of complete coats. If you're carrying out a re-paint where the old surface has just been flatted rather than taken back to bare metal, then skip the etch coat as it can attack old paint.

Applying etch by spray gun is

ideal for practising your technique. Set up the gun according to the instructions which came with it. You'are aiming to get a spray pattern which is shaped like a thin, upright rugby ball, with an even distribution of paint within it. Keep the gun roughly one hand span from the surface, and as parallel to it as possible, so you follow the curves of the frame or panel exactly. Always trigger the gun before starting across the metal and do not shut it off until you have passed over it on the other side. Try to overlap each pass by 50 per cent. There's lots of information online, giving hints and advice on how to apply paint, but there's no substitute for practice, and the etch and primer coats are non critical so use them to build up your confidence.

PRIMER

If the etch coats were very thick it might be an idea to lightly sand them back before applying two coats of high build primer. This is designed to

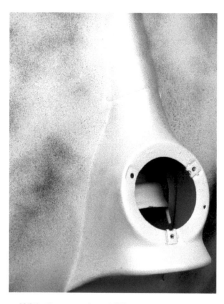

With the metal and filler clean, apply a couple of coats of primer. Once that has dried, use aerosol satin black to lightly coat the surface; it will flash off quickly. Next, use 600 grit wet and dry paper, well wetted, and flat the surface just enough to remove the black guide coat.

Any defects which sit lower than the surface such as holes in the filler or heavy sanding marks from the filler stage will now clearly show up black against the lighter primer.

These small imperfections can be filled using stopper (cellulose-based versions are best for home use). Stopper is a very fine filler which can be applied very thinly, especially if you use a soft foam applicator, which will allow you to follow contours very closely.

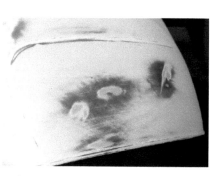

Once the stopper has fully hardened, overnight preferably, it needs to be sanded with 600 grit wet and dry. Once done, the surface of your scooter may look like a patchwork quilt. Here, for example, you can see bare metal, the brown of the etch, the white of the primer, and the light grey of the stopper.

fill minor imperfections, and can be flatted back to a level surface with 600 grit wet and dry paper. Use clean water only to lubricate the paper at this stage.

SEALING SEAMS

Sealing the tunnel-to-floor gap is shown in the pictures. It's not original obviously, but done with care the end result is unobtrusive, and will prevent water getting into the frame cavity. It's also a good idea to seal all the panel joints in the engine bay on the underside for the same reason; as discussed in the frame chapter. Always use a dedicated automotive sealer. Silicone sealant sold for domestic use might appear financially attractive, but it can react with steel and accelerate rusting, which rather defeats the object. It will also cause havoc when you try to paint over it.

A coat of stone chip on the underside will also give long-term protection for a scooter used in all weathers, but make sure that it's compatible with the paint you intend

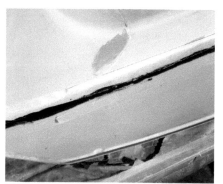

The join between the floor and the central tunnel can be a problem. Rust begins unseen in the gap then stains the paintwork over time when the scooter gets wet. Sealing the gap is a good idea, and, as long as it's done discretely, it will be almost invisible once the scooter is painted. Start by running masking tape along the top surface of the central tunnel, and then along the floor, as close to the gap as possible. Apply a thin bead of automotive sealant, and make sure it has fully entered the gap between the panels.

to use as a top coat. Finally, give consideration to using a wax based corrosion inhibitor injected inside the frame cavity after painting; aerosol versions are available.

PRIME AGAIN
This final priming session can be done with standard primer; a couple of coats should be enough. Flat off once more with 800 grit wet and dry, then clean throughly. Wiping over the surface with a tack rag will get rid of any small particles of dust, and leave the surface ready for the colour coats.

TOP COATS
The ratio for cellulose colour coats is 50/50 thinners to paint. Apply three or four coats, then, for the final one, up the ratio of thinners to 65 per cent. Use a measuring stick or graduated cups to get the proportions right, and use top coat thinners rather than standard. If painting in damp conditions try to find anti bloom thinners, although this is getting harder to track down now. The technique for

Use dedicated automotive sealant, it will not damage the metal and will be compatible with most paints.

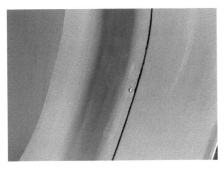

Pull the tape away carefully whilst the sealant is fresh, and you'll be rewarded by a very thin bead filling the gap perfectly.

Now apply a further two or three coats of primer to your stoppered and filled frame. Once dry, use 800s wet and dry paper, well wetted, and with some hand soap added to further reduce the cut of the paper. Flat the entire frame again. Make sure to keep your fingers at 90 degrees to the direction of travel to prevent introducing lines into the surface. Clean the surface thoroughly with more of the blue paper, making absolutely sure that all of the flatting debris is removed. The frame is now ready for the top coats.

Mixing cups and a dedicated stick are useful when preparing the gloss paint for the top coat, particularly as the markings help maintain the correct mix ratios, although a good eye, a clean glass jar and a thoroughly degreased steel ruler will do the job nearly as well.

Gun distance now becomes more critical, a hand's span is about right. Aim to keep the surface of the paint wet, but don't linger in one spot or runs are a real possibility.

When painting the tank make sure that the filler hole (and the tap hole if you're going to be painting the underside, too) is carefully covered with masking tape or you risk paint debris getting into the fuel system once the scooter is back on the road.

Small parts, like the clutch-side headset tube, will need to be masked off and supported to allow access to the underside.

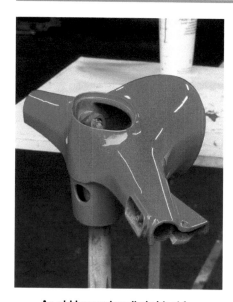

An old broom handle is ideal for supporting the headset, but make sure that it's secure or air pressure might cause it to spin, or even fall off, as you work.

The chances of getting a perfect surface straight out of the gun is pretty slim with cellulose, especially when applied at home.

Plastic adhesion promoters can be bought in aerosol form. Without them any paint you apply will flake off very quickly.

applying top coats is exactly the same as outlined in the etch section earlier. Gun distance becomes more critical, though, as the paint should go on 'wet.' If the gun is too far away from the metal the surface will look dry and matt. Be careful to maintain the correct gun distance on corners and curves, or there's a risk of uneven paint build-up and runs. There's no substitute for practice when it comes to paintwork, and the main benefit of cellulose paint is that it dries quickly, and any defects can be rubbed down and recovered if required.

FINISHING TOUCHES
Having left the paint surface for a couple of days, it needs to be closely inspected. It will probably have dulled slightly, and there may be specks

Once the surface of the paint has been flatted back, apply some brazing paste to a small area at a time and, using a buffing machine, bring up a real shine. Always keep the head damp and constantly moving, or there's a risk of burning through the paint.

of dust trapped in the surface. Use 1500 grit wet and dry paper (very wet, and cut with a little plain hand soap) to gently flat the surface back to a uniform dullness. Apply brazing paste to a small area and polish with a buffing machine, borrowed or rented, as, although it's possible to do it all by hand, it's arm-achingly tedious. Do not flat off the paint close to panel edges or places that are difficult to reach with the machine; hand buff the original surface in these bits. Once the shine has been regained, apply a good quality polish with soft cloths.

PAINTING PLASTIC
This is really only a concern for 50 Special horncasts. Plastic parts fresh out of the packet have a greasy residue which must be removed (using panel wipe). Use paper towels and change them a couple of times during the process. Aerosol adhesion enhancers can be used before applying primer. Speak to your supplier about your proposed paint system, and read the instructions on the can of your chosen product, as they do vary.

Chapter 6
Trim

FLOOR RUNNERS

Floor runners are available in kit form, and prices (and quality) vary. They were fitted by rivet at the factory, and so, if complete originality is required, a set of concave-nosed drifts to do the job is available from a German parts supplier, as is a tool (which looks and operates a little like a valve spring compressor), to make the job of fitting them easier. The main drawback with using a drift is that the force needed to squash the rivet means a lot of hammer swinging close to your scooter's newly repainted surface. Pop-rivets could replace the original hammered variety, but have to be fitted from the top to allow room for the rubber inserts. The alloy is narrow on Smallframes, so double-check that your rivet gun's nose will seat fully without damaging the sides of the trim. Other possible alternatives are shown in the photo sequence.

If you're restoring an early 50N, the floor strips are rubber, but without the alloy trim. They have small protrusions on the underside which push through holes in the floor to secure them, with a couple of rivets at each end to finish the job.

The trim on the main tunnel can either be two runners matching the floor, or a larger mat secured by two trim panels at the side. These panels can be attached using small, stainless self-tapping screws or by pop-rivet.

The rubber insert usually comes as one long section. Measure each runner in turn, making allowance for the end caps, and trim very slightly oversize with a sharp craft knife. The small amount of extra material can be compressed easily, and will allow for shrinkage, which inevitably happens once the scooter's in use and exposed to the elements. The edge of the rubber can be lubricated with a little silicon grease to encourage it to slide into place. Leave the end caps loose until the rubber is fully in place, and then tighten down. It's possible that the rubber will bulge slightly where they meet the caps, if it is unsightly trim the top of the rubber with a knife, with the excess material gone the fit will be noticeably better.

Rubber overmats were fitted to some models, and remanufactured versions (in black and grey) can be sourced easily.

The old floor runner rivets can be ground off if the scooter is going to be repainted. If not, remove the old rubbers from the alloy trim and drill the rivet heads to release them.

Quality of replacement parts may be an issue. This set, which was of European origin, came with one runner of an incorrect length. This, obviously, required cutting and re-drilling; not a major problem, but irritating.

If the end cap holes are obscured by moulding flash (they often are), these will need to be cleaned. The floor runners will come with short and long soft-rivets, the latter for the end caps. Unless you're determined to have a factory-fresh look, there are easier methods to attach the trim.

Drill to suit your chosen method of attachment. All this work should obviously be done before painting, to minimise the chance of scratching the new surface.

A quick layout will probably reveal that the curvature of the runners straight out of the packet bears only a vague resemblance to the shape of the leg shields.

Many scooter shops sell M4 bolt sets with countersunk heads for floor runner attachment. They are fine, but 3.5mm (5.5mm spanner for the nuts) are worth considering. They sit lower in the head of the end cap, though, which may not appeal.

If sourcing your own fittings, such as this machine screw, choose ones with low profile heads. It isn't critical, it just helps when fitting the rubbers.

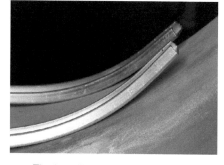

The long flat sections are easy to straighten, the short curved ends slightly less so. Mark with a pencil the point at which the curve needs reshaping, then slowly bend by hand, re-checking against the leg shields regularly as you bend. The final shape does not have to be absolutely perfect as the tension introduced by the fittings will pull the runners tight to the bodywork.

Once happy with the position and fit to floor, mark where the holes will need drilling, assuming you've changed the floor. If not, you'll already have lined it up with the originals on the initial trial fit.

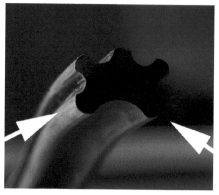

The floor rubbers come with three top ridges and two which fit into the alloy channels. The rubber can sometimes prove reluctant especially on the curved sections. Use a screwdriver and gently push the edge into the runner if it's reluctant to slide in to place. Work slowly, or you may tear the rubber.

The main benefit of using M3.5 nuts and bolts is that the visible fittings at the front of the leg shield are smaller and neater. Alternatively, you could use original rivets at this point, and nuts and bolts for the rest.

LEG SHIELD TRIM

The original trim on V-Series scooters was a one piece alloy moulding finished in a dull, corrosion resistant coating. Replacing this requires the use of a special tool (shown in the picture sequence). Using the tool is straightforward in principle, but the reality may prove otherwise. If the tool is reluctant to roll as designed, use it to crimp the back of the leg shield in small sections, lifting the tool away and reseating it as you go. Once done the inside of the trim will look lumpy, use the tool again and it will probably now move as the makers intended. Roll it all the way around and re-examine. It may be necessary to do it all again to achieve an acceptably smooth finish.

A popular alternative to the original fitment is the two-piece screw-on type of trim, often referred to as Cuppini regardless of the actual manufacturer, which is quick and easy to attach. Cuppini also does a double leg shield trim in chrome for a more custom appearance. If either of these appears attractive to you, it's worthwhile brushing some wax-based rust inhibitor on the inside of the trim before fitting, as they can corrode quickly. Similar trim is also available in stainless steel, for a more weather-resistant finish.

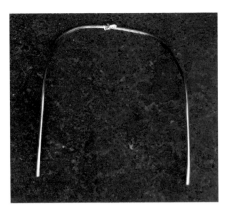

Original leg shield trim comes as a one-piece fitting, which needs a roller tool to crimp it to the leg shields. It's large and delicate, so make sure it's well packed if you're buying mail order.

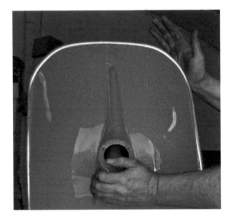

Start the fitting process by slipping it onto the leg shields and tapping it down with the heel of your hand.

For the central tunnel end caps, self-tapping stainless steel screws are a quick, easy, and not unattractive solution.

Once in place, the new bits really give your scooter a lift, and the contrast brings new paintwork to life. In this case, a non-original placement of the runners has been used, they should sit over the edge of the floor, but a slightly inboard location gave the preferred look.

The fitting tool is relatively expensive, so borrow one if you can unless you intend doing other Vespa restorations. It relies on squeezing the two handles (white arrows) together by hand. The operating heads (yellow arrows) do the work. The black one maintains the shape of the trim, while the white one bends the inner face of the alloy against the leg shield.

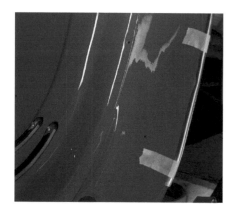

Before using the tool, double-check the trim is seated correctly all the way round, and use some tape to hold it in place so it doesn't move as you work.

The principle is straightforward: pull the tool around the leg shield whilst squeezing the rollers together.

Other options include a semi rigid plastic chrome effect/black strip, which knocks on by hand, or a similar style but in soft rubber, which is also easy to fit as it simply rolls onto the lip of the leg shields (and is available in a range of colours). Whichever trim is chosen, make sure that you check its relationship to the floor runners; the original trim for example goes on first, with the last section sitting under the runner, the screw on type usually has cut-outs to go over the runners so can be fitted after they are in place.

Once again, just like the floor trim, the base model 50N differs from other scooters as it was supplied with no leg shield trim.

MUDGUARD TRIM
The more upmarket models came

with a dull alloy trim fitted to the mudguard. This was held in place by clips on the underside. A wide variety of replacements are available, from standard to custom. Even the copies of the originals tend be more highly polished than those fitted from the factory, though. Double-check the distance between the locating pins before ordering a replacement; there are differences between models.

STANDS
Replacement stands are available for virtually all models. Up to 1972 the tubing was 16mm in diameter, increasing to 20mm thereafter. Both sizes are available in black, bare metal, or chrome finish, with an option for a reinforced version if required. Chrome versions may appear attractive but the quality of plating can be extremely poor.

Centre stands rust, bend, and wear at the pivot points, so replacement may be the best and simplest option. They come in two diameters, 16mm and 20mm, check before ordering brackets and feet.

New brackets are readily available, but if the old ones are re-useable then stick with them. The ones here came with a new stand and were misshapen, and the holes were incorrectly drilled. The replacements were marginally better, but still required the mounting holes to be elongated as the stand fouled the frame. If the originals are going to be reused, check the inside operating surface for signs of wear. If they're fine, a wire brushing and a coat of wheel silver will make them ready for reuse. A liberal application of white grease on fitting is a good idea.

Stand springs weaken with time. Replacements and their frame clips are cheap. The traditional method of locating stand springs is to use a piece of sturdy cord and pull the spring back onto the clip. A safer alternative may be to grasp the flat section of the spring with a pair of locking grips and use them to pull on. The clip is slotted into the frame, and then the spring pulled back and hooked on to it.

New stand feet are cheap and should just slide in place with a couple of taps with a soft-faced hammer. If they are tight, gently warm them with a hot air gun or immerse them in boiling water for a minute to soften them.

BADGES

Leg shield badges come in a variety of shapes and, more importantly, locating pin dimensions; check carefully before ordering. Originally, these were secured by 'mushrooming' the backs of the pins. Some copies available now rely on the same method, others use circular clips. If the original method is being used, one of the drifts for fitting floor runners can double up to secure badge pins. A small blob of Sikkaflex or similar on the rear of the badge before fitting will take up any slack, as it can sometimes be difficult to get them really tight. Horncast badges, hexagon or shield type, may need fixing with Sikkaflex, too, although self-adhesive versions are an easier option, but they are thinner than the originals.

Leg shield badges can come with solid pins like this, or loose rivets. Both have their heads mushroomed over when fitted originally, and so these need to be ground off to release them (arrowed).

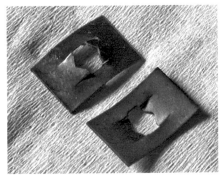

Later versions will also have pins, but are secured with small metal clips which can be levered off with a screwdriver.

Adhesive badges with the old script can be bought in two sizes; the smaller one probably being the most suitable for a Smallframe.

Just about every variety of badge is available for your Smallframe ...

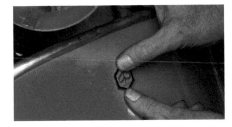

... including self-adhesive versions, which makes fitting very simple. Peel back the protective film on the back, position, and stick in place.

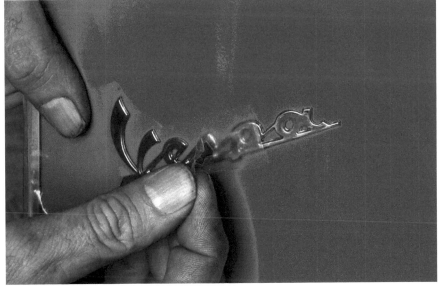

Simply peel off the backing paper, align the badge, and push it on. Gently rub over the surface with a cloth to make sure that it has stuck properly, then peel away the top layer of plastic as shown.

SPEEDOMETERS

For many markets the 50cc Smallframe Vespas were supplied without a speedo. If the headset had a hole for one (and not all did), then a rubber blanking plug was used to cover it. New plugs are available, in round and square versions. The majority of scooters fitted with a speedo had a small round version, the square versions were on the 50 Specials from 1969, to match their rectangular headlights, and an oval speedo was fitted to the Primavera. Replacements can be sourced if the original is beyond restoration (which is fortunate as they weren't reliable and suffered from discolouration due to sunlight). Spare parts to rebuild speedos are rare, and professional restoration is unlikely to be cost effective, although speedo faces, glass, and chrome rims can be bought for some models, but they may cost more than a replacement unit. Prices for remanufactured units vary with quality, as ever, and also with the markings on the speedo itself. All attach to the headset in a similar manner – via a metal bracket with a rubber seal under the speedo head to prevent water ingress. Spanish Smallframes use a clamshell-shaped speedo similar to that of the large frame Sprint model, but it's shallower. Sprint replacement glass and chrome edge trim will fit.

HORN COVER

On late 50 Specials the horncast was made of injection-moulded plastic and secured to the frame by by screws. Although plastic can be successfully welded it usually goes brittle after a few years, and as replacement parts aren't too expensive, they're probably the best solution if the item is cracked or damaged. Some regard the original moulding ugly, so it's possible to buy a 'retro' plastic version that is bonded to the leg shields with adhesive. The alternative is to weld in a metal version, as shown in the pictures.

RUBBER PARTS

Virtually all the rubber parts required for restoration are available individually or as part as a complete bodykit. Some of these items were relatively expensive, but as more suppliers have entered the market the price has dropped, so a full kit, for example, will cost about the same as a new tyre. Shop around for the best prices.

Handlebar grips can be sourced in original form or in a multitude of colours. Most Smallframes have 24mm diameter grips, and are 125mm long, although some early 50cc scooters were 5mm shorter. Replacement grips vary range from the semi-rigid vinyl to really soft, thin rubber. If fitting the latter, a little lubricant (some people recommend aerosol hairspray) on the inside of the grip will not go amiss, as they tend to be naturally sticky and are too soft to hit on the end without them splitting. Fit them with a twisting motion. The harder plastic versions can usually be simply knocked on with a soft-faced hammer.

Thin handlebar grips must be fitted with care, they split if you try to knock them on.

Rubber parts , such as this horn seal, can be sourced in non-standard colours. Contrasting colours, like white against orange, as in this case, can be striking. Using stainless screws for items like this makes a lot of sense.

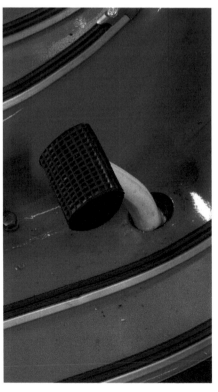

Brake pedal rubbers are a safety as well as a decorative consideration. The long section of the pedal is inserted into the rubber, then the other end pulled round to secure it.

SEATS

Smallframe seats can be a single
saddle coupled with a luggage rack,
a dual seat, or a sportier single with a
slope back as fitted to Italian market
50 Specials. Remanufactured copies
of all types are readily available
and represent a quick and easy
solution to a tatty seat. Individual
springs, both the uprights and the
longitudinal strips, can be bought to
repair metal-sprung double seats, but
finding replacement foam is the main
problem, as the original goes hard
and crumbles over time. Replacement
covers can be found if your foam is
reusable.

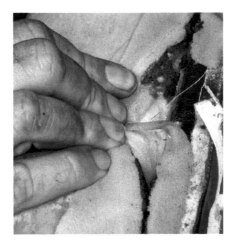

Seat foam rots, and, even when in good
condition, may have been glued to the
base, making removal difficult. Note the
rust trapped under the foam.

The securing latch may need some
work to make the seat secure. The
locating pins on sale are not all the
same size either, although they are
meant to be, so the combination of a
wide hole and a narrow pin can be a
frustrating situation to have to sort out.
Leave the front mounting bolts slightly
loose while you adjust the seat fore
and aft to square it up to the pin.

New seats come in many styles and just
as many prices. The general quality of
most is perfectly acceptable.

Chapter 7
Electrics

OVERVIEW

The Smallframe electrical system is pretty basic (verging on crude), and, unfortunately, received many detail changes throughout production. Virtually all models were six-volt with an unregulated power supply, the only exceptions being the 50 Special with electric start, which used two six-volt batteries in series, and the V100 Sport, with a single 12-volt battery. Both scooters are rare.

WIRING LOOM

If a complete restoration is being carried out, then replacing the loom is a very good idea. The original wiring will almost certainly have deteriorated, and fault finding can be difficult when so much of it is hidden inside the frame. Standard and custom looms are readily available new, off-the-shelf, and at reasonable prices. However, they're pretty simple, and can be replicated easily at home, if you prefer. Your local auto electrician should be able to supply all the necessary wires, in the correct colours and gauge, along

with some loom tape. If you're buying a loom, however, make sure that the sub-loom for the headlight comes as a separate piece; it makes threading the loom much simpler.

Fitting the loom is straightforward in theory; it can simply be pulled through the frame from the back to

the front using a guide wire. In reality, it tends to stick where the internal frame supports narrow the hole. A combination of pulling and gently twisting from side-to-side will usually get it through. If it's really stuck, however, don't put strain on the loom; pull it back a bit and try again.

Replacement looms are readily available for standard and modified scooters, and at reasonable prices.

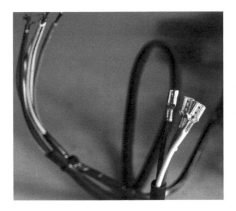

Good quality versions will come with connectors already crimped in place, where appropriate.

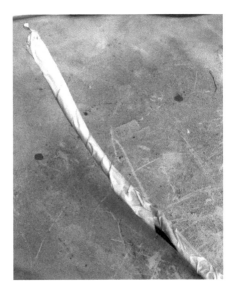

Tape up the end of the loom that will attach to the headset, as it will help its passage through the frame. Lightly greasing the surface can help, too.

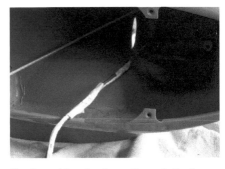

Feed a guide wire down through the frame from the top, and attach it to the taped end of the loom. Pull the guide wire gently while pushing the loom from inside the frame at the same time.

Once the wiring appears at the top of the frame, remove the tape and pull the loom through by hand.

The horn wires should be lightly taped to the main loom during installation. Watch for their arrival through the horncast hole as the loom passes.

The same applies to the brakelight wiring, although it obviously has far less distance to travel before it's in place.

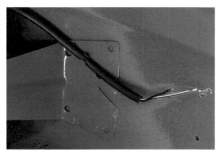

The wiring for the rear light passes through a small hole in the back of the frame. There should also be a fold-over clip to hold it up and away from the back wheel.

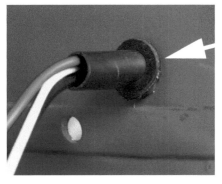

A rubber grommet is used to protect the wiring, make sure that it is still present and in good condition.

MAKING CONNECTIONS

There's no doubt that the best way to add connectors is by soldering them in place. However, unless done well, this method can also create problems. Many restorers prefer instead to use crimped connections. Some looms will come supplied with loose ends to be added once everything is threaded in place; but make sure to use the correct crimping tool. Don't be tempted by cheap versions. They tend to be pretty useless, and the resulting poor connections will only lead to frustration when you're trying to sort out subsequent problems.

Wiring diagrams are freely available on the internet. The combination of colour coding and numbered switch connections should make connecting everything pretty straightforward. If you've bought a complete loom, the supplier will usually help out if you're struggling with a particular issue.

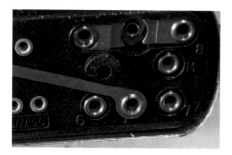

When connecting the handlebar switch, the screw contact points are all numbered, which makes life easier.

Depending on the scooter you may need to fit two wires into one socket, in which case each wire may need to be thinned before they will both fit in place. Insulate any exposed wiring with tape before screwing the switch back in place.

HEADLIGHT

The headlight glass on Smallframes can be removed if the bonding agent around the edge is scraped away. Take great care not to apply any side loading to the lens itself as you remove it; they can and do crack. Replacement lenses, bowls and bulb holders have been remanufactured for virtually all models, including the oblong versions fitted to late 50 Specials, and complete units are

available, ready to slot in. Cheaper replacement lights may have plastic lenses, which are obviously less weather resistant than glass and may not be a good option if a 12-volt conversion is being considered given the extra heat that will be generated. Some Smallframes came from the factory with only dipped beam fitted, no main, so check before ordering a replacement; they take a P26s bulb, usually of 15W. Scooters with both beams use a BA20d type bulb, usually 25W/25W.

Headlights come in two sizes, and are referred to as 105mm and 115mm – although, in reality they are actually a little bigger.

The internal silvering suffers as the steel headlight bowl rusts away underneath it. New ones can be easily sourced ...

... as can bulb holders. The quality of replacements can be patchy; expect to make some fine adjustments to ensure reliable contact with the bulbs.

The bulb holder pushes into the back of the reflector, and is held in place by two clips (arrowed), which simply pivot and push into place. Quality problems may be apparent once again, and they may be too loose to keep everything in place, so more judicious bending may be required; but be careful, the clips are brittle.

The headlight bulbs have side plates (arrowed), which fit into slots in the bulb holder and twist to secure, the sidelight has two small pins, and also twists into the holder.

TAIL LIGHT

There were several types of rear light unit fitted during production. Reproductions can be bought as complete light units, and also as replacement lenses. They are all pretty much interchangeable if an 'older' look is preferred. In many markets, 50cc Smallframes used under moped regulations were not obliged to have a stop light fitted. For use on today's roads, though, a change to a version with a stop light makes a lot of sense, and is a legal requirement in the UK.

If the original unit is to be reused and the plastic has gone dull, try rubbing it with a little mild paint brazing paste, or toothpaste; either should help bring back some shine to the surface.

Most rear lights have festoon bulbs fitted – 6V/5W for the tail light, and 6V/10W for the stop light, the latter being the physically larger of the two. Late Primaveras and ET3s with the PX type lamp may have twist socket bulbs, BA15s, same wattage as previous models.

Several types of tail light assembly were fitted to Smallframes. They are all pretty much interchangeable; the older style, pictured, being a popular swap for a more 'retro' look.

The unit is held by a single machine screw and nut. Make sure that the rubber gasket is in place between the light and frame. The wiring may need to be adjusted to allow the assembly to fit properly, as it can get in the way.

The wiring is simple, an earth and two feeds to the bulbs. The larger festoon bulb is the stop light, the smaller the tail light. Later type rear light assemblies will have round bulbs in sockets, similar to the pilot light in the headlight.

SWITCHGEAR

The majority of V-range scooters had a switch block on the right-hand handlebar fitted with a push on metal cover, although the functions and position of buttons varied. Later 50 Specials had a plastic version which followed the same basic layout. On models with indicators there was a circular housing on the left-hand bar, with a plastic lever mounted on the underside. Repairs to any of these units is almost impossible, so replacement is the best solution.

Standard switches for all models are available, as are upgraded versions for 12-volt conversions.

The chrome switch cover pushes over these machined slots to secure it. This point of contact also provides an earthing point to allow the kill switch to work. Some paint may need to be removed here for it to function properly; check once the scooter is assembled and running.

HORN

Remanufactured horns can be bought to replace corroded or non-functioning ones. If the original is six-volt and reusable it will still work with a 12-volt conversion, as it's not in use long enough to come to any harm.

Replacement horns suffer from quality problems, chrome versions can be very poor and rust rapidly.

STATOR PLATE

Age and heat are the main enemies of the stator plate, resulting in crumbly wiring and worn out coils. Look for discolouration on the copper windings, and bend the wiring gently to check how brittle it has become. Checking resistances is possible if you know your way around a multimeter, but for long-term reliability consider wholesale replacement. The best budget option is to hand it over to someone like Beedspeed (if you live in the UK) who will check it out, rewire it, give you a price for any additional work needed , then carry out the job. The magnets in the flywheel also weaken over time and there are very few establishments able or adequately equipped to re-magnetise them anymore, so consider the 12-volt option discussed later.

Replacement three-coil plates with points can be bought, as can electronic versions for the ET3 model. Ignition and lighting coils are available for earlier models, there are several varieties so check with your supplier to make sure you have the correct one; plates are usually identified by the number of coils fitted and the wires exiting from it. An upgraded supply coil for a better spark can be bought for 50cc models, and will help starting.

Ignition points come in at least five versions: long and short; with and without central pin; and the compact PX type fitted to some 50 Specials and V100 Sports. The points gap is 0.35mm to 0.4mm for most versions. If you have an ET3, the points are replaced with an electronic pick-up box which is the same as the PX type. It's held in place by a single screw which is usually very tight, and its single wire is soldered in place. These units are usually very reliable, but if the scooter suffers from any unusual misfires or hesitation, then it's a prime candidate for replacement.

Flywheel magnets weaken with age. Approach them with a screwdriver, the pull should be strong once you get within an inch (25mm) or so.

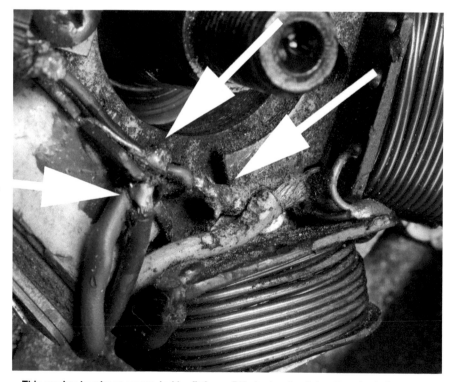

This engine has been upgraded by fitting a PK electronic stator. Despite being much newer, it's still suffering from crumbling wiring and poorly soldered connections. Automatic replacement is the best solution for aged electrics.

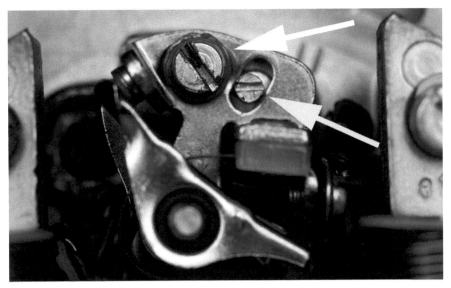

There are many types of contact breaker points available, but all will be secured to the stator plate by a screw (white arrow). This version has an adjustment screw (yellow arrow) with an eccentric cam for setting the gap. Most versions simply have slots to allow the use of a screwdriver blade to do the same job.

Condenser wires may be soldered in place, or may have the wire (and there may be two) permanently attached depending on model.

The points will have insulating washers and blocks to prevent shorting out. Take a note of how they are fitted during removal.

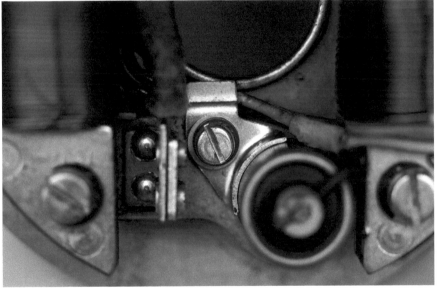

The condenser may be a simple push fit into the plate, or may have a securing screw that has to be undone.

Points replacement should be automatic during a rebuild; they are cheap. These ones are clearly bent (how such damage takes place can be mystifying sometimes). Clean the contact faces of the replacements with some fine abrasive paper before fitting as they usually come with a protective film over the faces.

Condenser replacement is advisable, as just like the contact breaker points, new ones are cheap.

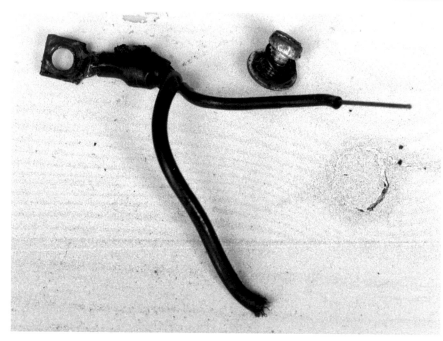

As mentioned before, brittle wiring can be an issue. This section looked fine when attached to the points, but simply fell off the stator during removal ...

Coils were not particularly reliable when new, so automatic replacement makes sense; there's no point leaving any weak links on a rebuilt scooter.

in. The ET3 coil is a CDI unit, with four connecting wires, and is similar to the type fitted to PX models.

... as did the wiring on the coils. Do not take a chance on your electrics; they were built down to a price when the scooter was new, so replacement and/or an upgrade is the best solution in the long run.

SPARKPLUG/HT LEAD/COIL

On standard engines an NGK B6HS or equivalent should perform perfectly well. If the scooter is used for longer high-speed runs, use a cooler-running B7HS. The HT lead is an automatic replacement part on a rebuild. It simply screws into the coil, which has a threaded post built in to it. The plug cap may originally be a simple brass fork inside a rubber sheath, or, on later models, a metal 90-degree cap. The latter are unreliable and should be replaced with a modern plastic or rubberised version.

The coil may be internal on some Smallframes with a lead directly to the sparkplug. On the remainder there will be an external version mounted to the engine case, it will be obvious which type you have. Replacement external coils may come with an HT lead built

12-VOLT CONVERSION

Given the amount of money you're likely to have spent on the restoration already it would make sense to splash out a little more and convert to 12-volt, and preferably go with electronic ignition at the same time. This will enhance starting, which can be a weakness of the Smallframe models, improve the lights, and probably squeeze a few more miles out of gallon of fuel as well.

It's possible to have 12V lights and retain the 6V points setup just by changing the lighting coils. Better, though, to buy a complete conversion kit from your chosen parts supplier, but ensure that it will fit the crank in the standard V-range motor; some are designed to work with later, larger-taper cranks. The conversion will also require a regulator, a new light switch, brakelight switch, bulbs, a CDI unit, and some changes to the wiring. However, if you decide on this upgrade at the beginning of the restoration process, a dedicated wiring loom to suit can be purchased and fitted ready for the upgraded electrics.

This is a PK electronic pickup used in a 12-volt conversion. Constant ignition timing plus good long-term reliability are a real bonus once your Smallframe is back on the road.

If you change to 12-volt, then a regulator is going to be needed. A 3-pin PX version is fine, and readily available, but is a little bulky to hide away. More compact aftermarket versions can be sourced which can be mounted in the tank cavity; check with your supplier.

Chapter 8
Wheels

RIMS

Quite a few different rims were fitted to Smallframes over the years, but they basically fall into two distinct types. First came the pressed steel rim with a solid centre and a detachable narrow outer, as shown in the line diagram at the start of the picture sequence. This rim was initially nine-inch, which is an unusual size with a very restricted tyre choice today. Remanufactured nine-inch rims are currently available, as is a conversion rim to change to the ten-inch wheels fitted to later models.

The second type is a hollow-centred rim which attaches to the outer edge of the brake drum. Just to complicate matters, this was also available initially as a nine-inch wheel, later becoming ten-inch by adopting the same rim as the large frame Vespas. The nine-inch version attaches at four points to the drum, as can be seen in the photograph in the Introduction to this book, the ten-inch at five points. A conversion rim is also available, should originality come second to functionality in your list of priorities.

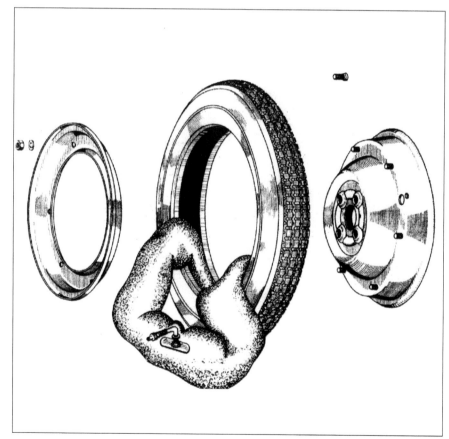

In the early years, most Smallframes were fitted with a solid-centred wheel secured to the hub by bolts.

Replacement rims are available from many manufacturers. Italian versions are widely regarded as the best quality.

For 10-inch wheels tyre choice ranges from sporty to classic, and even includes off-road knobblies.

Push the tyre onto the deeper rim half with the inner tube valve hole in it. Feed the tube in and push the valve stem through the hole.

If the original rims are to be reused, check them carefully for rust damage. Heavy pitting where the steel is curved from the original pressing may mean replacements are needed. Examine the rim mounting holes, too, as they can become elongated if they've been insecure at any time in the past. Genuine Piaggio rims are more robust than the aftermarket versions currently available.

TYRE REPLACEMENT

Smallframe tyres are narrow, and, despite split rims, it can sometimes be a struggle getting them on. The picture sequence shows the use of hand soap to lubricate the side walls, but a tub of proper fitting paste is not too expensive, so it may be worth considering.

Buy good quality inner tubes, some cheap Far Eastern versions are very poor. It really isn't worth saving pennies in this area.

Add a little air to just give the tube some shape, this will help prevent it getting trapped between the halves as you tighten things. Don't fully inflate it, though, or it will make fitting the other rim half much harder. Make sure that the valve is sitting square in its hole.

Rims come in original grey plus a variety of non-standard colours and finishes. If a particular colour is required, the supplied coating can be simply rubbed with a Scotchbrite pad to key the surface ready for paint.

Before starting to fit the tyres, lubricate the lip with a hand soap solution. It will help enormously when trying to get the tyre onto the rim.

Lubricate the tyre lip on this side, and push the other rim half down. It will require some effort but once the first nut is screwed on a little, it becomes easier. Don't forget the split washer under each nut.

Once all the nuts are tightened – and it's best if they are done in a criss-cross pattern rather then just working around the rim – over inflate the tyre slightly to make sure the bead is fully in place. Deflate, and then pump back up to the correct pressure. Try 18psi in the front, 22psi in the rear as a starting point, then fine-tune to suit your weight and riding style once the scooter is back on the road.

Replacement rims may bulge between the fittings as the steel is thinner than original rims. This obviously disappears when the rim is bolted to the hub.

Ready for fitting, but that may not be simple either, as replacement rim halves often don't line up perfectly. They may need some minor adjustment before they sit on the hubs properly.

STUD REPLACEMENT

The drum shown in the pictures is actually from a PK Smallframe which came after the V-range, but the stud replacement process remains the same for both types. Once the new stud has been fitted and the locking compound has gone off, stake the back of the new stud with a sharp chisel, two blows at 90 degrees to each other should be enough, which will also help prevent it from unscrewing.

Models fitted with solid centre wheels secured by four bolts are more of a problem when there are damaged threads. If it's just the bolt threads that have worn, then replacements are cheap. If it's the threads that are cut into the plate which forms part of the axle assembly front or rear, however, then that represents a greater problem and considerably more expense. These plates are shallow, but may be re-cut with an appropriate tap, but as they are a safety critical item anything less than perfection isn't really acceptable, so a replacement assembly will have to be sourced.

Hub studs often break off and can also suffer from rust where the rim has been sitting.

It is also common to find damaged studs replaced by a bolt screwed into the hub.

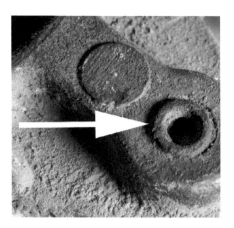

The back of the stud will either be mushroomed, as shown here, or there will be a cross pattern where the end has been staked over.

Either way, select a drill bit which fits into the back of the stud and drill off the end.

Try locking two nuts together on the rim side and unwind the old stud. It can be very tight, though, and it may be better to use locking pliers to get a good grip on it; this obviously destroys the old stud, as shown here.

Dab some locking compound onto the threads of the replacement stud which will be screwed in to the hub.

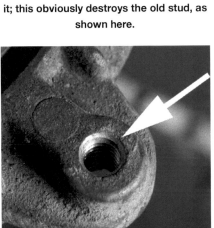

Check the internal threads carefully, but they should be fine if you've just removed an original stud.

Use two nuts locked together to screw the stud into place. Don't try to remove the nuts until the locking compound has had time to go off

Also from Veloce:

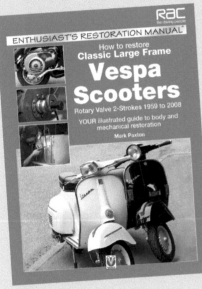

How to restore Classic Largeframe Vespa Scooters
– Mark Paxton

Investigates the reality of Vespa restoration in detail. The author strips and rebuilds largeframe models in his workshop, outlining common problems and how to address them. Aimed at the do-it-yourself enthusiast and featuring 1100 clear colour photographs, it is an essential step-by step-guide to the complete renovation of your beloved largeframe scooter.

ISBN: 978-1-845843-24-3
Paperback • 27x20.7cm • 160 pages • 878 pictures

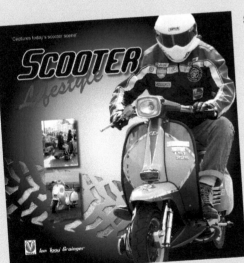

Scooter Lifestyle
– Ian 'Iggy' Grainger

Scooter Lifestyle will capture the imaginations of past, present and future generations of scooter riders, and guide the reader through the scootering way of life and all its factions, giving a unique insight into the modern scene and all its diversities – warts and all! Includes interviews with well known scootering personalities, over 150 colour photographs of award-winning custom scooters, best-selling scooter models, rallies and events. This book is a must-have for anyone interested in these fashionable, fun machines.

ISBN: 978-1-845841-52-2
Paperback • 25x25cm • 128 pages • 380 pictures

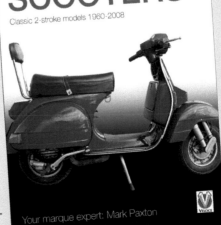

Vespa Scooters
– Mark Paxton

The two stroke Vespa's initial purpose was to provide low cost transportation to the masses in the 1950s, but it evolved to became a symbol of burgeoning youth culture. The history of this phenomenon has

been well documented,
as has the subculture that
surrounds it, but there has
been no previous attempt
to provide a guide to
buying one of these classic
scooters. This book will help
ensure that you avoid the
main pitfalls and end up with
your very own slice of La
Dolce Vita on the driveway.

ISBN: 978-1-845843-34-2
Paperback • 19.5x13.9cm
64 pages • 99 pictures

The Essential Buyer's Guide

Piaggio
SCOOTERS

All modern two-stroke & four-stroke automatic models
1991 to 2016

100,000+ COPIES SOLD THIS SERIES

Your marque expert: Henry Willis

Piaggio Scooters – Henry Willis

Among the most popular and well used
scooters in the world, automatic Piaggio
and Vespa scooters mix Italian cool with
everyday usability. They're also cheap to
buy and run – but what should you look
out for when purchasing a scooter? This
book explains every consideration, from
the point of choosing a bike through to
buying your very own scooter.

ISBN: 978-1-845849-92-4
Paperback • 19.5x13.9cm
64 pages • 90 pictures

– and ...

Caring for your scooter – Trevor Fry

This book is aimed at the rider who wants to do his or her own basic scooter maintenance and servicing without the need for in-depth mechanical knowledge, or a technical manual. It covers areas such as oil, brakes, tyres, transmission, electrics, etc, allowing the owner to address the most regularly serviced items without forking out for additional costs. Illustrated with full colour photographs throughout, and featuring clear, easy-to-follow instructions, this book is a must-have for scooter users.

ISBN: 978-1-845840-95-2
Paperback • 21x14.8cm 80 pages • 89 pictures

The Lambretta Bible – Pete Davies

A year-by-year, model-by-model, change-by-change record of the world's finest scooter from Model A to the GP 200. The story doesn't end there, though, the focus moves to machines prepared and built by Lambretta Concessionaires. The

book ends with a look at the main British dealer specials of the 1960s. Essential reading for Lambretta enthusiasts.

ISBN: 978-1-787111-39-4
Paperback • 25x20.7cm •
160 pages • 200 pictures

Scooter Mania! Recollections of the Isle of Man International Scooter Rally
– Steve Jackson

Offers a complete history of the event including competitors' and organizers' personal experiences, plus the controversies and difficulties experienced by the Rally Committee in what became a remarkable 20 year chapter in the history of scootering sport and tradition.

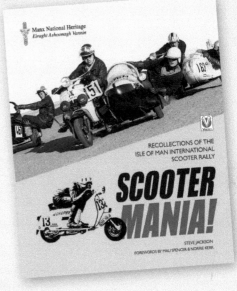

ISBN: 978-1-845846-48-0
Paperback • 25x20.7cm • 128 pages • 180 pictures

Vespa – The Story of a Cult Classic in Pictures
– Günther Uhlig

The history of Vespa, from its beginnings to the present day, clearly arranged, understandable for all, and, above all, describing even the tiniest detail in an unprecedented form. An illustrated chronicle, with all the information needed for complete understanding of the culture of Vespa.

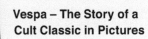

ISBN: 978-1-845847-90-6
Hardback • 26.5x23cm • 252 pages • 475 pictures

Index

Shock absorber
  front 66, 71
  rear 88
Sparkplug 108
Speedo 54, 100

Stand 98
Stator plate 14, 35, 106-108
Studs
  cylinder 12, 36
  wheel 112, 113

Tail light 105
Tyres 111, 112

Wheels 111
Wiring 102, 103